i am kami

My dance through darkness into light

Kami Kay

Author photo by: Jen Brown
www.ofstardustandearth.com
(http://www.ofstardustandearth.com)

ISBN: 978-1-951503-69-7 (Hardcover)
ISBN: 978-1-951503-70-3 (Paperback)
ISBN: 978-1-951503-71-0 (Ebook)

Authorsunite.com

To Sam and Sav,
I never lost you, I only lost me.

To my brother and sister,
Thank you for loving me through this messy life

To Kat and Robin,
Thank you for always giving me a place to lay my head

And to all of my Luv Thing friends, thank you for all
of your support. You have all carried me through with your
unconditional love, goodness, and grace.

For all of the beautiful friends who left this world without
your voice being heard, this is for you.

Special thanks to Joelle Hann, Hannah Wallace and
Laura Brittain for helping to bring this story to life.

Sending love,
kami

i am kami

*"**Kami** is the Japanese word for a god, deity, divinity, or spirit. It has been used to describe mind (心霊), God (ゴッド), supreme being (至上者), one of the Shinto deities, an effigy, a principle, and anything that is worshipped."*
Wikipedia contributors. (2021, November 2). Kami. In *Wikipedia, The Free Encyclopedia.*

PROLOGUE

Finally, my energy had shifted, and I was falling back into the flow of life. I had already spent plenty of time going up and down, around and around on my personal rollercoaster of pain. I had gone over all the "would-have-should-haves" long enough. I knew one thing for sure—I had been asleep long enough. I had tried to mold myself back into this 3D society most people called life, but I'd hardly been living. I was just passing the time away trying to exist. Trying to prove to myself and those around me that I was sane. But hadn't I been sane long enough? And what really is the definition of sanity anyway?

I was finally ready to dip my toe into the magical waters of life once again, and without being called crazy. I had recently started reading tarot cards again and was actually being paid to do so. After twenty-five or thirty years of studying all kinds of spirituality, I finally felt ready to share this part of myself.

Even just thinking of this just now, I immediately bow my head in humble gratitude, letting the universe know how grateful I am for the opening to help people. This kind of sharing through card reading and storytelling is as much for me as it is for them. I love to give them a glimpse into a possibility that they had not thought of, to open them up, to wake them up. Not the "woke as fuck" wake up, like that of many newbies on their spiritual path, or that of the "woke political party." No. No judging, but just *saying* you are woke as fuck may mean you are still so very asleep.

What does it mean to be awake? It's something I have been contemplating myself for years now. It really means to pay attention, to be aware. To really see what is going on around us. To realize that what we see, what is happening, is actually what we are all co-creating, together, as one divine movie called life.

I was so happy to be pondering these thoughts once again, yet nervous about keeping my energy contained. I texted a friend to see if she could meet me at barre class. She texted back that she couldn't because she was in Mexico. It seemed most of my friends were in Mexico these days. Once again, I wasn't making the invite list, no longer included in the inner circle. I no longer had the means, or a man—just a couple of the necessities needed, I guessed, to make the list. I sat down in my quaint, little Zen garden to open the mail.

That was a mistake, I thought while opening the five notices from the IRS making a claim that I owed back taxes. I quickly calculated the sum—$250K. I was unable to substantiate the records from my last year of brick-and-mortar business, circa 2009, when everything had still been on paper. The IRS stated that I owed them for the business expenses, plus inventory of my last year in business. I had closed my brick-and-mortar clothing business while still doing $350K annually, and my expenses had been $185K then. The bottom line had still been pretty good, I chuckled, realizing how good that still sounded. But I had never recovered from the recession, which had decreased my sales by fifty percent. Even after the dust had settled, I couldn't keep up with the inventory needed to fill a store to capacity, allowing it to thrive. Even in its last days, the numbers had still made it seem like a pretty solid small business—the American dream—and I had lived it. Now, in my garden, I shook my head at the ridiculousness of all this—the 2008 recession had ruined me financially. It had happened over ten years ago, though. Time to wake up and take back my life.

I went to barre class alone, but what else was new. I had been doing everything alone these days. I tried to forget my outside life and lost myself during class, then started thinking about my stupid taxes again. I laughed out loud when Lisa, my instructor, said, "You can do this posture all day long, even while doing your taxes!" It was the end of October—who else was thinking about taxes? I laughed and lost myself again, then kept laughing as I listened to the lyrics singing about "wearing your heart on your sleeve." I had built my business, named "It's a luv thing," on just that, sayings about love on T-shirts, and especially the ones with the "heart on the sleeve." After almost fifteen years, the heart on the sleeve T was still my best seller. I smiled at myself in the class mirror, admiring my new eyelash extensions. Once my signature, I'd often commented that the only thing fake about me were my lashes. I hadn't had them in years; they certainly had not been in my budget lately.

Then Lisa said, "Look through your eyelashes!"

What? I laughed again, thinking, "Oh, you are a funny universe! Okay, whatever, eyelashes are good." I was enjoying myself—a tarot reading gig again that night in Rancho Santa Fe. Young rich kids—let's see if I could spread some magic and goodness. Moving my hips as instructed, lashes good, I was making a comeback. Mean girlfriends—whatever. I thought I should start taking the hip-hop dance class with them. Yes, I was fifty-four, but hey, I still looked pretty good, I thought as I looked at myself in the mirror—not skinny, not fat, and definitely not tall. But I still had a pretty good ass, thanks to barre class. Finally, asses were in. Funny though, I'd really never had a problem with shaking it. I mean, didn't my friends know I'd been voted "most likely to become a Solid Gold Dancer" in high school? Again, I laughed at my own entertainment.

Why were my feelings so hurt? Why did I want to dance and show that I still had it? Maybe I should try out for the performance group at my dance studio, I thought—dress up and really share who I was on the inside.

I laughed again as I looked in the mirror at my wrinkles. I had earned them all. I had no desire to prove myself anymore, to dance or perform. I had done that already, and that ship had sailed. Besides, I had become such an introvert lately, barely leaving my apartment, alienating myself for years now, hiding from the pain and judgment I'd felt from everyday dumbasses, and the feeling had been mutual. Going to my workout classes was one of my only escapes.

After class, I waved goodbye to my friend, the phone ringing as I walked out of the small lobby where I sometimes did pop up shops. Since Lisa, who owned the studio, had just started the next class, I offered to answer the phone.

The woman on the other end said, "Hi there! I am looking to hire five dancers for a Solid Gold theme party next Saturday and wanted to know if your studio had any dancers available." I couldn't help but laugh out loud. Oh, universe, you do crack me up!

I suppose it is time to tell my story.

So, who am I?

i am kami, and this is the story of my personal journey through the dark waters of life. I learned the meaning of my name years back on a lovely trip to, yes, the mental hospital. Not your typical place to find yourself, but that is what happened. Afterwards, I had to go home and google my name for myself, to believe it.

My name means God, the hidden energy and essence in everything.

Over the years, I have learned that we are all just that: the reflection and essence of God, expressing ourselves in this lifetime through our thoughts and actions, if we only just stepped into it. If we believed it, we could create our own heaven right here on earth, instead of the hell that is often created when we live in the dark energy of fear.

I really feel it is time to drop the labels, which only come from a lack of understanding. It often makes life easier to just label someone, separating them from ourselves rather than seeing them and accepting them for who they are in any given moment.

Why is it that this vast separate-ness is something that we have learned to accept as normal?

I hadn't felt normal in years. I often woke up, usually in a sweat of panic, heart racing, body enveloped in fear as I often wondered how I might make it another day without killing myself.

What was the way anyway, and why was it so uncomfortable?

What was in between the looney bin and suicide? To me, it felt as if there was nothing, absolutely fucking nothing.

OCTOBER 19, 2020
ONE YEAR LATER

I opened the mail. Yep, there they were, all the IRS letters again. They sure were consistent, "as is the universe," I said out loud to myself as I climbed onto my big red velvet couch to write, wearing my newest accessory, a bright pink cast. Writing was not such an easy task with a broken wrist, which I'd gotten from falling out of my new mobile clothing boutique. The old funny me would have called this "forced change." There were no more barre classes, or boxing, or other distractions to keep me from completing my book. It wasn't so funny, I thought as I reflected on my last entry—a year ago, exactly, to the day. Opening the mail on the couch, not caring about the contents, I was overwhelmed with sadness about what tomorrow would bring and how the events mirrored last year's writings exactly. Chills ran up my spine as I typed with my one hand, and the hair on my arms stood up to tingle, just so.

Tomorrow, I'd attend a small memorial service for a friend's daughter, twenty-two years old, who had died of a fentanyl overdose. Another friend's daughter would turn twenty-four tomorrow, and she would spend her twenty-fourth birthday in the mental hospital. Exactly what I had written about one year ago: "What is in between the looney bin and suicide?" My heart broke that I hadn't done more, grown more, and shared more. Why hadn't I helped to create a healing center or the thriving community I had always dreamed of living in? Where was this place where people could feel loved, nourished, supported, and cared for unconditionally in this journey called life?

The day's date,1019 in numerology, broke down to 119.

One hundred and nineteen, the opposite of 911, always meant emergence to me. This would be the opposite of emergency, yet I hardly felt emerged, and I felt far from enlightened. My goal, however, is to share my story, in hopes of sparking some awareness and change. Somehow, I just KNEW there was a better way of living in this life, in this reality. It could be a beautiful reality that we are all capable of co-creating. I often say, "Wherever our focus goes, our beauty shows."

And at times, it was just the opposite.

1

I WAS SO FUCKING HIGH

NOVEMBER 2, 2007

They tested me for everything, only to find a very low amount of THC, which stays in the blood for up to thirty days. But I wasn't high, not that kind of high anyway. I was out of this world high. High on life, on love, on God. Oh, I was high all right, high on me. The connection that I was experiencing was so strong, so wild, that everyone was certain I was on drugs. But I wasn't. I was just manifesting as fast as I was thinking, learning to control the brain—or giving into the control of the brain. Was it mind before matter, or matter before mind? I loved to contemplate such things, but I really wasn't sure. Kind of like which came first, the chicken or the egg? What I knew for sure was that the energy flowing through me was more than I could handle. I left the house shortly after I woke up and called my friend to see if she would pick me up.

As I walked, I started to get anxious with the enormity of what I was experiencing. My marriage was crumbling, and now I was channeling. These two things were not a good combo. I couldn't go back home and face my husband. So, I called one of my best friends, the one with the celestial name, who knew I could be out-there at times. I asked her to pick me up and check me into a hotel. She lived a few small beach towns away and had two small children. She couldn't come, though, because she didn't have anyone to watch her kids.

"Oh, well, that's easy! I'll just send you a sitter!" I said with enthusiasm, and then hung up. I walked, I channeled, I began to cry and laugh at all these questions I had. They were being answered as I asked them. It was like being in two worlds at the same time. I was sitting with a group of sages in another dimension and walking the neighborhood in this one. The sages are serious, but funny. They are like me in many ways, like different aspects of me, yet I know they are not me.

I walked to the Self-Realization Fellowship Temple, then walked to the Meditation Gardens as I conversed with who I believed to be my higher self. "What would you give up for love?" was the question my guides, or my higher self, posed. I instantly dropped to my knees on the dirt overlooking the cliff to the ocean.

Humbly I said, "Everything, everything." That was my immediate response, taking off my jewelry, my prized sweater, offering them up as if to an altar that wasn't really there. I hesitated, "Except for my children!" I screamed. Then I sobbed.

Somehow, I knew in my soul, in some way, I had just offered them up.

I really had no idea.

My friend called me back, wanting to know what was going on.

"Why?" I asked.

She said that her in-laws had just shown up on her door-step, asking if she had any errands she needed to run, because they would love to watch the children. The fact that they had shown up unexpectedly scared her.

I tried to explain, "It is just energy. If you go directly up, you can tap into the unmanifested field quite easily." I was dropping my creative manifestations like rain drops, and her in-laws—who were in touch with her and her children—obviously got the message and showed up.

"It's just energy, don't worry," I told her.

She wasn't buying it.

She showed up and found me in the Self-Realization Fellowship Meditation Gardens. I mean, where else would you go to talk to the real guides, to get the real answers? I loved the founder of the temple, Paramahansa Yogananda, and loved being in his lush gardens. I felt his love in return. If you wanted to know the big answers, why not ask the "big people"? That was my thought process, anyway. So why not visit him at his house, which also sat on the cliff overlooking the ocean at Swami's beach? It wasn't just him that I was chatting with, for he held such revered company. I was also talking to Jesus, Mary Magdalene, Buddha, Quan Yin, Ganesha, and several other great sages and archetypes for whom I did not know names. They were talking to me about the importance of keeping your body clean (meaning the food you eat) and your mind clean (how your thoughts really create your reality), and about being mindful of your words. All of these things make up our physical reality, the world in which we see and live. They talked to me about the brain being an intense tool that we could use to create a beautiful heaven, right here on earth.

My celestial friend wasn't so happy about the way I was acting. Soon after she arrived, she also started crying as I talked to her about balance and meditation while we walked down the hill past Yogananda's house.

"See, it's like this," I said as I jumped up on the four-foot-high brick fence and started scaling the thin brick wall surrounding Yogananda's house in my snow boots. I was balancing myself as he told me that anything was possible if you could find the balance. I also learned from him that there was no such thing as bad and no need for judgment, shame, or guilt. That even the "bad" in the world is all perfection, offering spiritual evolution, or "soul growth," for those creating it.

My celestial friend became even more afraid as the people from the temple came outside. They were concerned I might fall from the wall and probably also wanted me off the sacred grounds and private property. Okay fine, I was ready to go. Celestial said she had lost her car keys, so we could not leave, but I knew she was lying. We waited there on the driveway of Yogananda's house while she cried and called more of my friends. I was still chatting out loud with my higher self and all my guides. I was so happy for the intense connection I was experiencing. These wise, magical souls were laughing at me and shaking their heads with love, like you do to small children the first time they think they really know something but don't. They wanted to let me know I was not in tune with my body, that I was not grounded. I had not learned to bring my energy down into my lower chakras. I was not embodied. True and true again. I knew my lower chakras were pretty fried. I was afraid to go there, to feel the pain that sat deep in the core of myself. I didn't understand exactly what my guides were sharing with me—something about how sex in our culture had become so shameful, keeping us from connecting to the root of our Kundalini Shakti, the base of our energy body, which is extremely powerful. This same shame, fear, and guilt kept many of us from rising up to our highest energy potential and knowing. This was not only true for me but for most women and men.

"No, no, I am not afraid, I can do it," I answered back to my guides while putting my hands down my pants to find my pussy.

A look of horror and confusion passed over my celestial friend's face as she witnessed this. It was also quite obvious she had never masturbated. (Or maybe just not in public.)

I had never learned to masturbate. I'd always thought the word alone was so ugly, why would anyone ever want to do it? I had not learned to love my true inner essence. Could this be because of the shame and guilt surrounding the idea of masturbating?

The first time I had heard the word, the bishop of my church called me into his office. I also felt shame along with it.

"Kami, are you masturbating?" he asked.

This body shame never went away. It kept me from really knowing my body until well into my forties. Why was there so much shame around women enjoying sex? This piqued my curiosity. Sex was at the forefront of almost all marketing, yet masturbation wasn't openly talked about with my friends, or anyone, really, that I knew of at the time. I had always looked to men for sex, rarely looking to please myself.

My first attempt would, of course, have to be publicly on the sidewalk of Paramahansa Yogananda's house, in front of my sweet friend. And let's not kid, it wasn't sexy. She was one of my best friends, but this would be the end of our tight friendship. She and our friend Kiley Boo, who had recently become besties, never spoke to me again after this incident. I lost so much that day it was absolutely soul crushing. While I was experiencing the essence of life in all its awe and splendor, filled with so much knowing and oneness—just like that; it was gone, over.

It was gone in one swoop, as if someone had swiped up all the jacks before the ball dropped, this divine intervention and my beautiful life. Just like that, it was over.

2

THE PICKET FENCE IS NOT PERFECT

NOVEMBER 2, 2007

I had almost flown out of bed earlier that morning—I was so excited to see the magic of the day. I had been elated, and curious to see how the universe might reflect back to me some of the goodness and love I knew were available to me. I peeked out my bathroom window at an eerie coastal fog as the sun glistened through my favorite room. Oddly enough, my bathroom was the only place I really felt at home in our custom-built house by the beach. I often spent countless hours meditating while soaking in the clawfoot tub, which sat next to an overstuffed green chair where I read. Next to the chair sat the darling antique vanity that I had designed the whole bathroom around. I watched as the morning sun filtered in through the bathroom window in rows of rainbow colors. This was my retreat, my odd yet peaceful sanctuary, I thought, but not today. I didn't dillydally as usual. I put on some sweats, fur-lined boots, and my favorite long, hot pink sweater with bright gold trim. It was chilly for Southern California; there was a crispness in the air as I opened the gate of my picket fence. The dew of the morning made everything sparkle as if by magic. I could see the rainbow glow around the trees and the plants. The water droplets glistened thick on the grass and made me feel as though my engagement with the plants made them sparkle even more. I let them know how much I loved and appreciated them as I walked by and blew them kisses. I loved the world, and I loved Mother Earth so much. I shivered as I felt the love in return, or was it just a cold day? I wasn't really sure. We lived a block from the beach in North County, San Diego, in the darling house that my husband, Dave, had built for us. As soon as I shut the gate that day, I knew it wasn't my gate. I felt as though it wasn't my house, not anymore, which made me shudder. I resided here, but somehow, I knew it wouldn't be for long, as I walked out of my "perfect-on-the-outside" picket-fenced house.

The picket fence that surrounded our house looked perfect on the outside, but on the inside, our house felt lonely and sad, absent of love and kindness. This time, when I closed the gate to our picket fence, I somehow knew that things would never be the same between my husband and me. I really had no idea just how good my life was, or that all of it was about to come tumbling down.

My poor husband. He gave me such a confused look as I walked out of the house.

I told him, "I'm great, I found a new spiritual teacher, and everything is gonna be great, just great. Don't worry, I am fine." He shook his head as if he did not understand or even know who I was. The distance between us had become so vast. We shared the same space, but the energy between us was thick, dark, and painful. I usually couldn't wait to get space between us.

Today was different, though—I was feeling so alive, so amazed by everything in nature. I was me, but a better me—a bigger, more connected me. I felt so connected to the earth and the world around me. I knew somehow things were different. I could see things vibrating with color and dimensions, unlike anything I had ever experienced before. I needed to sit with this, sit with the information that was downloading into my brain. I was answering my own questions before I actually finished forming the questions.

I knew I was seeing and feeling God's essence in everything.

I left the house in my eccentric get-up, with a cream beanie that had a big feather and a rhinestone patch. I had one in cream and one in black. I swore someone in my family hid these favorite beanies of mine so I would quit wearing them. I wore them all the time. But this time would be the last. I started walking, not really knowing where I was going. I was almost in full meditation at this point, but a walking one—I was in a walking dream state. I would think of something, and it would happen. I was envisioning looking for my next house. Where would it be? I knew it was close by—I could feel it. A place to find peace, with plenty of sunshine for plants and flowers, which reminded me of my mom. I was wishing for my mother as I turned the corner and saw my daughter Samantha's second grade teacher. She looked and sounded so much like my mother that it was uncanny. I had joked with her about this a few years earlier when I was a regular volunteer in her class. I'd been very involved with Sam's teachers at the time. Having a child with cancer will turn any mom a bit neurotic. Not only was Sam sick with cancer, but she also had no hair and had a puffy belly from the steroids. I checked in on her at school often to make sure she was happy and adjusting well, and to make sure the other kids were being nice to her.

Here was this beautiful teacher, one of many who took extra care of my daughter. She was laughing while having coffee at one of the local sidewalk cafes. I must have looked at her funny as I told her that I'd just been wishing for my mom. Her smile vanished when she saw the look of pain and confusion on my face. I had no idea where I was going, but I just kept walking. I wasn't feeling myself. She left her friends and walked with me for a bit. As Sam's teacher, she shared in the pain and fear that surrounded a child with cancer. Even though Sam was now in fifth grade and perfectly healthy, the trauma to us all had left a fresh scar.

When I was with Sam, I was so afraid she might somehow see the fear in my own face. The fear of losing her. I had given endless pep talks to whoever was going to see her, making sure their face held no pity, no fear. My kid was sharp as a tack, and I did not want her to see fear on anybody's face, especially mine. I would sternly put on my poker face, reflecting back to her that she would be fine. I was adamant about it. I guess that's why my scar, my pain, was buried so deep.

The teacher and I shared a few stories about Sam and how strong and determined she was, then I said goodbye as I hugged her. She said she loved me and would pray for my family and me. Truly, we had the best teachers for the children in our small beach community. Everyone knew everyone here, but the trade-off was that everyone also knew what everyone else was up to. That's the way it was in a small town.

It wouldn't take long for rumors to fly around of my fall from grace.

PART TWO

3

BAREASS NAKED

SEPTEMBER 1983

"You came bareass naked—you can leave bareass naked!" That's what my mother screamed as she chased me down the street when I was seventeen. Hardly the way most high school graduates left home, but then again, I was definitely not like most. There had been no college tours or even talk of college in my family; it had not even been an option. But that wasn't going to stop me from leaving home—I was moving out, no matter what. It was the first time I had ever run away, and I certainly had zero plans to go back.

This would become a pivotal point in the deep dive of finding my own way. For a long time, I hadn't felt at home in my small town in the state of Utah. For a graduation gift, I'd received a hope chest from my parents. A hope chest was something given to most young Mormon girls there. It was a wooden chest, usually made of cedar, somewhere you put your homemade quilts, embroidered pillowcases, and whatnot to take with you to your marriage. It was a far cry from being a probable replacement for what many traditional cultures used as a dowry, and it was certainly not something I wanted.

13

The last thing I wanted was a hope chest. My hopes and dreams were not of making babies and staying in Utah, as my mom requested me to do. My mom and I, always in a battle of wills, quarreled often about whether this or that was truth because "they" said so on television. Who were "they" anyway? This "truth" that always came down from "them" always felt so fake and coerced to me. I was a curious kid and determined to get to the bottom of who "they" actually were. This kind of thinking always intrigued me, and I wanted to know more.

I did want to go to college, I thought, but I guess I didn't really. I hated school, but I wanted to do something to escape the confines created by my mother and small hometown. I had no plans of getting married and having kids right away, which was my mother's wish but not mine.

College was not an option at the time as my mother worked outside of town for a road construction company and only came home on weekends. And we just couldn't afford it. It was my responsibility to watch after my younger sister, Keri, and hold down the fort. My mom rarely came home, even on weekends.

I never looked forward to her coming home anymore anyway. There would always be hell to pay for something: the house wasn't clean enough, the laundry wasn't finished, her beloved flowers were not watered. One weekend, she came home after being gone for a couple of weeks, and her flowers had all died. It was hot in the summertime in Utah, often over one hundred degrees, and the flowers needed daily watering to keep them from wilting. I had obviously forgotten a time or two. Now her treasured geraniums and purple-and-white alyssum were all dead. She then beat me with my own tennis racket in front of my two best friends, Kate and Rachel. I hardly remember any of it, only that I covered my face and yelled for her to not break my new racket. My friends, though, remembered the incident quite vividly.

She wasn't always mean, of course. But as a kid growing up, I never felt she loved me. I don't ever remember feeling connected to my mother, and I always felt like I was trying everything to earn her love. I tried to be perfect in every way I knew in order to get her attention. I got fairly good grades; I was cute and funny and even popular. I took dancing lessons because she wanted me to, and I also knew to get out of her way when she was mad. Other times I would do just about anything to impress her, but nothing worked. I felt she was harsh, and she had a cold heart when it came to me. I was mushy, and, like most kids, wanted affection and hugs—to be tucked in and kissed goodnight and treated as if I were important and special. Yet this affection was just not something that came naturally to her—she would say, "Good night" and close my door, and that was that. No hugs or "I love you." She left notes daily of chores I had to do before I hung out with my friends or even did homework, which my parents never asked about anyway. I never felt as though they cared—they just wanted the chores done and Keri, who was five years younger, looked after. I don't even remember how old we were when she became my responsibility. But I do remember cooking for the first time, home alone. I was making Keri some soup and then calling my mom, worried it was filled with bugs, only to see it was just pepper. We were somewhat on our own from a very young age. My parents rarely ever asked questions about how I was, and I often felt they really didn't care.

When I was six years old, my mother couldn't even be bothered to have a real conversation with me when she told me that my "dad," Greg, wasn't my biological father. The subject came up because of a few meetings with a new grandfather.

An old man had been picking me up after school and taking me for ice cream. After going for ice cream several times, he mentioned that he was my grandpa and then dropped me off at my house, knowing exactly where I lived. Confused by this, I wanted to know why he was *my* grandpa but not my siblings' grandpa too?

My mom sat on the bathroom counter of our newly built 1970s split-level brick house, and while putting on her face, told me that my dad was not my biological father.

"What about Mike?" I asked.

"What do you mean?" she asked.

"My brother, Mike, is he my brother?" I wanted to know.

I loved my brother so much, though we fought like crazy, as his teasing never ceased—but I loved him dearly. The thought of him not being my brother threw me into a panic as I sat on the closed toilet seat, hanging onto every word as my mother shared the story of my meager existence.

"He has a different father than yours, but yes, he is your brother," she said.

I sat watching my mom apply her makeup, rouge, eyeshadow, fake hairpiece, and false eyelashes—none of which she needed—as she continued to tell the story of how I came about. All my known life I'd thought I had a brother, a sister, a mom, a dad, and a shit-ton of the best hick cousins you could ever have. I was devastated. Now I feared none of these cousins were really mine. My last name wasn't even real. That is, it didn't legally belong to me since my stepdad, Greg, never had adopted me.

I tried to absorb this earth-shattering news, to let it sink into all six years of myself, but this was a lot for a first grader. Mom couldn't even stop for five minutes and give me her focused attention on a subject that took the light right out of me.

I think this was when the seed of hate for my mother may have been planted.

She proceeded to tell me the story of marrying my biological father, as if it was just any unimportant story.

She said, "I met your father, Alfred—we dated for a while, and I ended up pregnant. He was in the service at the time, stationed somewhere in Colorado. Shortly after I became pregnant, he was in a car accident. He hit a parked police car on a bridge while driving drunk. The crash resulted in the policeman's death, and your father went to prison for life. The man picking you up for ice cream is his father, and the kindergarten teacher who has been giving you gifts at your school is your grandmother."

I listened, completely shocked, while trying to digest this seemingly unreal story. I fidgeted, legs up, legs down, trying to make myself comfortable in my small body while still sitting on the closed toilet seat. I continued to twist my long blonde ponytail around and around, gazing at her as she continued to tell me more about my biological father.

"His parents, being the strict Mormons that they are, insisted we get married. So, that's what we did. I married your father at the Colorado State Penitentiary. I didn't think he would ever get out, and shortly after, I met Greg when you were a baby. He took you in and treated you as his own. Your biological father ended up getting out of prison early—he saw you once when you were less than a year old, and then he moved to North Idaho."

It was fuzzy after that. The confusion left me feeling lost, empty, and alone. I tried to comprehend what I had just learned. I ran downstairs to the basement of our new house, to an unfinished bedroom that would soon be mine. I climbed into the framed-out closet and cried, unable to swallow as I tried to control the loud sounds that crept out from deep inside my chest. This was the first time I'd really felt emotional pain like this, and it was just too much for me to grasp. I curled up on the cold concrete floor crying as I held both knees close to my chest, wrapping both arms tight around them, certain my newly cracked heart would just fall right out of my body if I let go. Right then I decided that was exactly what I needed to do. I needed to hide this painful part of myself. I let go of my knees and frantically started pulling at my chest, then wiping my hands on the wall of my soon-to-be closet, sobbing as I tried to wipe the pain from my broken heart. I didn't want to be me, why was this happening to me? I silently cried as I intentionally left part of my heart behind, releasing some of the pain, unable to carry such a large burden. It was just too much weight for a such a young girl. Soon the sheetrock would go up, then the paint and the yellow floral wallpaper that I had recently picked out. My secret and suffering would be safe there in the closet—nobody would know of my hidden pain and the deep open wound in which it sat. I had dozens of amazing cousins. They were the best part of my entire childhood, and now I didn't even belong to these people? How could they not be my people?

I really couldn't believe it. In the span of just one afternoon, the life I'd once known shifted completely. Flashes of my short childhood were trying to fit into my brain and adjust.

"My grandparents too?" I'd asked Mom. My heart had broken even more trying to make sense of this incomprehensible news. My world, as I once knew it, was collapsing. If Greg wasn't my dad, then two of the most important people in my life, my grandparents, were also not part of me. My head reeled, thinking about the best part of growing up in this small town of Mormons—that I was pretty much related to everyone.

The big family gatherings at my grandma's were the best—I have more than twenty first cousins. Thanksgiving was my favorite time. We would rake the leaves from the giant oak tree in front of my grandparent's house into the biggest pile of leaves possible, and then run and jump into them. When someone walked down the long sidewalk to my grandparent's house, one or more cousins would be hiding in the big piles of leaves, ready to jump out and scare the walker half to death. Fun and games were always on the forefront with my crazy cousins. My grandma was the absolute best; she could host a party of fifty like nobody's business. She was always in her tiny kitchen baking up something, bottling, or pickling the many fruits and vegetables we grew. In the fall we would also pick all the fruit, climbing the fruit trees and throwing plums at each other. Fun with my cousins just never got old. All the kids loved going to work with my grandpa on the farm, riding on the tractor or in the back of the truck.

I must have been about eight years old when he let me drive the hay truck, and I remember the brick that he put on the gas pedal to hold it down because I couldn't reach. I also had to sit on a pillow to see over the big steering wheel. The big, old truck didn't go very fast, so I didn't worry too much. I was always so excited to drive the giant truck through the field with my grandpa. I found it fascinating that sometimes we had corn, sometimes hay, and sometimes wheat, changing the fields as well as the soil. My grandpa explained that by changing the crops each time, it also added nutrients back into the soil, enriching it in order to grow the best crops.

Farm life was not always easy and never boring: once while hauling hay, my cousin Renae fell out of the back of the truck and then got run over by the hay wagon. She got two black eyes and a broken nose—she was lucky it wasn't worse. I also watched my grandpa put his entire arm into a cow, turning the calf so it could be born.

The worst family tragedy happened when I was quite young. I was sitting on the floor at my grandparent's house, coloring in a coloring book, when one of my uncles ran into the house screaming and crying hysterically, blood all over his hands.

He was screaming, "Mother, Mother, help me, help, what have I done!" Tears streamed down his face as he told my grandmother that one of his young sons, only two or three years of age, somehow had wondered off, then lain down in the tall grass. My uncle had been driving the giant hay swather, when he realized he had swept up his own tiny son. A hay swather is like a giant lawn mower, about ten feet wide and

19

a few feet tall, with extremely sharp blades to cut the tall hay stalks that our family farmed. My uncle was obviously quite beside himself with immense grief and disbelief. I will never not see his bewildered, pained face in my mind. I really don't know how he and his wife recovered. Maybe that's why they just kept having kids, almost a dozen in total.

My grandparents, who had very traditional masculine and feminine roles, seemed fascinating to me—they were always busy creating or crafting something new, all while taking great care of one another. Not only was my grandmother an amazing cook who made her own jams and jellies, she bottled peaches, pears, and plums. She also could knit, crochet, and quilt, and she was excellent at all of them. My grandma often worked on a big quilt in the large living room of her old brick house. A basket of yarn sat next to the sofa, full of her knitting. She was always making baby clothes; everyone wanted her baby booties and her embroidered pillowcases. She was a master homemaker and always wanted to teach us something new.

My brother and I moved into my grandparents' attic for a year or more while our house was being built down by "Doc's." Doc's was a piece of property my grandpa owned, named after some doctor who had originally owned it. Doc's was where my grandpa kept the cows most of the year, where they were branded and fed. One year they even barbecued Rocky Mountain oysters—a.k.a. "cow balls"—but I didn't eat any! Most of my cousins were there, and my mom and aunts brought tons of food, which we ate while we hung out on the back of the tailgate and watched my brother and cousins do their best to ride the young steers.

We were building our house just down the street from Doc's. While our house was being built, my parents lived in "Old Yeller," an ugly, yellow vintage trailer that they parked in my grandparents' huge front yard. My mom cleaned up Old Yeller. The things I loved most were the little, white eyelet curtains with the tiny pom-poms. It ended up being quite cute, and I wished there was room for me. My parents and new baby sister would live in the trailer, and my brother and I would live in the creepy attic with my dead uncle Bert's antiques. He had lived there years ago but had passed of old age or something. I was scared to be up there—I swear the place was haunted—I would rarely go up there alone. I didn't know how to deal with that kind of fear as a kid, so like everything else, fear got stuffed inside. Besides, living there gave me more time with my grandparents, so I guess I didn't mind too much.

I could hardly wait to live close to my favorite cousins, especially when there would be tall corn stalks to run through. We did this often, scaring one another in the stalks, pretending we were in the movie *Children of The Corn*. The tall brick house was finally built, and I would eventually have my own room downstairs in the basement next to my brother's room.

My grandma also cleaned the church once a week, and she would often take my cousins and me with her. It was so fun, and also kind of eerie, to run around the big, quiet church with all the little classrooms when nobody was there, playing hide-and-seek behind the big, heavy fabric curtains that hung in the auditorium. My grandma helped me write my first poem—for my first public speaking experience, also in that church. My grandma was so cool—she could do anything, and she was always so supportive and encouraging. Back then, I loved going to church and couldn't wait to get a CTR ring ("Choose the Right"). A CTR ring is something a Mormon girl receives at about eight years old, after baptism. It was green and shield-shaped, with the letters CTR on it. It was a reminder to the wearer to choose the right, to make good decisions. I loved everything about the activities and fun that our Mormon community offered. Even though my parents were not religious at all, I still went to church. My aunt Jolene usually picked me up on her way.

The first time I really remember tapping into my intuition and "knowing" was around the time I was seven or eight. That was the day I made Aunt Jolene leave in the middle of church to go home and rescue my mother.

I had gone to the bathroom during sacrament meeting, and for some reason, I peeked out of the auditorium window towards our house.

"We have to go home!" I frantically told Aunt Jolene as I ran back into the quiet church meeting. "My dad is beating up my mom, and we need to leave."

She believed me, and we quickly went home to a find a violent scene in the front yard, exactly as I had envisioned. My dad held my mom by her long, black hair—she was wearing one of her pretty, white cotton nightgowns, now torn and bloody, as he towered over her, screaming. Her face red from crying, she had marks on her arms and face where he had struck her, and her lip was bleeding. It was a bad scene, and I was scared. I always later thought that I had looked out of the auditorium window, through the cornfields, and into our yard. As an adult, though, I have looked through the window many times, and I definitely could not have seen them—the church is over a mile away from our house. After that incident, my siblings and I spent the next couple of weeks staying with Aunt Jolene, who was my father's sister and my favorite aunt.

In a recent visit with my aunt, I asked her if she remembered this incident, and I asked her why she had believed me. I had just been a child. Her answer was not what I expected.

"Of course I remember, Kami. You had never lied to me or ever given me a reason to not trust you, and I believed that at the time you were having an awakening." I hadn't realized my awakening had begun when I was so young.

My aunt Jolene was the strongest, most badass woman I knew, and I would eventually name my first daughter after her. She was the mother of five children, all of whom were my favorite cousins. We would be the first of many children she would take in.

When I found out Greg wasn't my real dad, I wondered if this amazing favorite aunt would still want me now that I knew the truth.

Did it also mean that I would have to take my picture down from the family tree with all the grandkids that proudly hung on my grandma's living room wall? The small golden frames were all connected together by little gold hooks on each oval frame.

This was the first time my reality, as I knew it, would all come tumbling down. But it certainly would not be my last. I felt I no longer belonged.

So it was really no surprise I ran away after high school. I wasn't expecting my mom to be home—she was rarely ever there. I had graduated, and all of my friends had left for college. One of my best friends, Angie, who had gotten pregnant, married, and then divorced—all while in high school—needed a roommate, and I was going. My mom did not agree to my moving out. But I had a job working as a cashier at a truck stop, and I was going to school to become a dental assistant. So I could pay for my share of the rent, groceries, and other expenses. I no longer wanted to live at home, being my mother's babysitter and housekeeper.

I had only spent one night at Angie's when I showed up at my old house to grab a few things for my new apartment, not expecting my mom to be home. But there she was, making her famous cinnamon rolls. She was an amazing baker, and her cinnamon rolls were my favorite. I acted like nothing was going on as I tried to gather some of my clothes and things from my room.

"Oh, no you don't," she said. "You do not get to take any of your things. I asked you not to move out, and you are not taking your stuff!"

I wasn't quite eighteen yet. I felt like an adult already as I had been home alone for years, and I could make my own decisions. We had a blowout fight, and with two cinnamon rolls in my hands and nothing else, I ran out of the house and down the street while my mom chased me. She yelled like a crazy woman as she ran after me.

"You came bareass naked, and you can leave bareass naked!" Meaning I came into the world naked, and if I were leaving home without her consent, I would leave the same way I came, bareass naked.

And so, I did. Well, kind of, as I only left with the few clothes I had with me.

4

MORE WALLS OF REALITY
TUMBLING DOWN

My Church dedication had come to a quick halt after an unnerving meeting with the bishop when I was fourteen. He called me into his office for a check-in. I sat down in his plain, sterile-looking office, wondering why I was there, when he casually asked, "Kami, have you been masturbating?" Not knowing what it meant, and not liking the energy that came from him as he asked me, I quickly said no. Then he asked, "Kami, do you believe the Church to be true?" I wondered what was up with this odd questioning that felt more like instilled fear, and wondered why was this always a question in the Mormon Church. Someone was always pledging that they knew the Church to be real and true. Why did they always have to confirm it with each other? I always wondered if they were just trying to convince themselves by shaming and coercing one another. Otherwise, why would they have the need to constantly confirm it, if it were indeed the truth?

After my meeting with the bishop, I'd gone home and asked my mother what masturbation meant. Actually, it was how the question came about that really sent her into a raging fit. The fact that the bishop had been speaking to me about something so private and personal did not sit well with my mother. One bishop had already been to our door asking for a copy of my parents' recent marriage license to make sure they were not living in sin. She had let him know, and not in a kind tone, that when he came back with a copy of his marriage license, she would be happy to show hers—until then he should get off her porch. Then she slammed the door in his face, and he didn't come back. Now, this bishop had asked her daughter about masturbation? Oh honey, a few heads were certainly gonna roll. My mother was not one to mess with when she was angry—she didn't care if you were a bishop of the Church or not. I am not sure how the phone call went after the bishop talked to me, only that she said, "I gave him a piece of my mind!"

But I was still caught up in wondering what kind of gross thing he thought I'd been doing. Why had he asked me that? I wondered if he was asking other girls my age the same question. I was embarrassed and ashamed, vowing to myself that I'd never touch myself in that way. I also vowed to never return to Church or see that man again. I didn't feel safe there anymore and instead found comfort in my big group of girlfriends and Mark, my darling new boyfriend. It was easy to rebel against this strict Mormon upbringing, where people were either known as "religious" or "partiers." God forbid you had a glass of wine or coffee or had premarital sex, all of which came with a heavy label. I just didn't care for the labels, or the Mormon religion. Back then, I had always thought of myself as a good Mormon girl, despite my parents' two divorces from each other—once when I was in the fifth grade, which was followed by my mother's short and sudden marriage to someone else and an annulment before she remarried my stepdad a couple of years later. Of course, then I was seen as a black sheep in the community, coming from a divorced and broken home. I didn't care for the stigma that came with this new label. Even before my parents' divorce, though, I hadn't felt like I fit into this religion with all the rules and shaming. I was being judged because of my parents' marital decisions, and it hurt. I had always been fairly involved in the Mormon Church, where we were taught to find solace in the faith. I tried, until the judgement came down hard while my parents were divorcing, and I wasn't prepared for how much it would bother me, or my mother. Everywhere you went, people talked about "the Church": was he or she "active in the Church?" Was so-and-so "religious"? Everyone knew everything about everyone in my small town, where gossip was normal and judgement and shame were laid on thick. My parents were far from religious, and everyone in the town knew it. I don't even recall my parents going to Church much unless a cousin they cared for was getting baptized or blessed. Even at that age, I felt that God wasn't limited to being within the walls of a church, or behind an organized religion.

No wonder I felt such a pull to find a place to belong. To be loved for me, whoever I was. My curiosity about who I was ran deep. I had a five-inch scar running alongside my bikini line that nobody could really explain. There'd been talk of my having lived with my grandma Barb (my mother's mother) for quite some time as an infant. My mom had said a month or two, but my grandma had said for almost a year or more.

What new mother leaves her baby for over a year? I'd heard it was my balloon-shaped belly that had put me in the hospital as a baby. Was that my body's way of crying out for my mother? I can only imagine it now, as I send love to my baby self, picking her up and loving her, stroking her head that was flat on the back. I had always teased my mom that she must've never turned me over as a baby, because the back of my head was so flat. This comment always triggered her and sent her into a rage. I think we both knew it to be true.

After I ran away at age seventeen, we didn't speak for over a year, then I made a civil agreement with her to come and pick up a few things. I had decided to move to Idaho.

As it turned out, I couldn't make it on my own, and my biological dad offered to pay for my college education if I moved to North Idaho. We'd first met when I was eight years old, and I hadn't been too keen about it. I had missed out on Thanksgiving at my grandma's with all my cousins, only to sit at a stuffy Thanksgiving dinner to meet this man who was my dad. There was nothing fun about it. After that, we saw each other once or twice a year. I went for a ski trip for a few days in the winter, a week at his lake house, and water skiing in the summer.

When I moved to Idaho, I said goodbye to my high school boyfriend, Mark, who at that point was the love of my life. He was my first boyfriend and had been my best friend for the past five years. I loved him, and I had no idea what a great relationship we had—so pure, so innocent and sweet. We cared for each other, but I did not want to stay in Utah. The last few years we spent together were some of the best years of my life. Double dating with Angie and Rick, Mark's best buddy, driving all over our small rival towns, either in Rick's blue Bronco or Mark's El Camino—a.k.a. the pig truck—which he drove until he bought the big, brown Blazer. The Blazer was his prize. He bought big tires, added a roll bar, and painted it metallic brown with flecked gold paint that matched his long, perfectly feathered hair. We loved driving up the windy mountain roads. If we weren't skiing in the winter, we were checking out the changing fall leaves, crunching through them, or camping out in the spring and summer. Outdoors in Utah was amazing, and I took for granted the changing of the seasons: the spring wildflowers and the green mountains showering with waterfalls. Bridal Veil Falls was on the way to our hometown hill, Sundance, where we grew up skiing. The first time I went skiing was in the fifth grade, and I wore old-school lace up ski boots. We all rode the bus from the park to the ski hill on Saturdays when we took lessons in the morning and then had free ski time in the afternoons. Sundance was where I met Mark. I'll never forget him walking into the lodge, with his long, brown hair, smiley face, and freckles. He was tall and thin, with tight ski pants and a baby blue pull over powder shirt—he was too cool for a real ski coat. He carried his ski poles into the lodge like the hip guys did. He had an expensive new pair and didn't want them stolen, or so he said.

One look at his big grin and I adored him. We soon became best friends, and then after a year we started dating. We lost our virginity to one another, we went to prom together, skied together, and supported one another as both of our parents divorced. We talked on the phone or saw one another almost every day for five years. Then all of a sudden, I decided I was done with Utah, and I was done with the judgmental society of the Mormon Church. Utah did not feel like home now that all my friends had left for college. Angie's life was more together than mine, and Mark was talking about joining his dad down south in his construction business anyway. I would be alone. I felt like I had nobody, and I longed for something more. My life in high school had been so perfect and full of fun and friends. But it had all come to an end, nothing was left. Once again, I felt alone in the world and felt the call to do something different—a longing for more.

I just didn't know what.

5

BIO DAD

I'll never forget the look on Mark's face as he said goodbye to me. He sat on the tailgate of his Blazer, staring back at me as he watched my bio dad, Al, and I pull out of the driveway of my very first apartment. He was crushed—he felt as though I would never come back to Utah, and he was right.

But after just an hour on the road, I knew I was in over my head.

My "bio dad," which is what I always called him (just not to his face), had always been nice and generous and kind of dad-like. I mean, I was his only biological child. But this time, there was an unsettling, awkward energy between us. We had never really been alone before. His wife and kids were always in tow, and now being alone with him in his truck, the tension was weird and thick. He liked me, but not in a good way. I knew he loved me, and we had gotten along fairly well over the years. I tried to let the feeling go, to brush it off. It was a long drive to North Idaho, and maybe I was just nervous. We checked into a hotel, but neither of us could sleep. He got up in the middle of the night and got into my bed and tried to snuggle up with me. Maybe it was innocent, yet I could see and feel his erection in his tighty whities. I immediately pulled away, scared and disgusted. I hurried and got up and said, "Let's get on the road." He was distraught and kept looking at me funny the rest of the trip, probably wondering if I knew that his odd infatuation with me was out of line. I ignored it. My little car and entire small life were being towed behind us in a U-Haul truck and trailer.

I was looking forward to moving; some of my happiest memories had been on Coeur d'Alene Lake, cruising up the beautiful St. Maries River to my dad's cabin. The water would be so cold, refreshing, and so smooth, perfect for water skiing. I could hang on to the rope for what felt like hours. My dad would laugh, trying to get me to fall into the lily pads, knowing it would freak me out. There were shallow parts of the river where giant lily pads grew up from the bottom, their big leaves floating on the top of the cold water. I loved skiing over them, but to fall into them, with the slimy vines entangling your limbs and skis, always freaked me out.

I hadn't seen my bio dad much over the past few years—I was too busy being a teenager. I'd had a boyfriend, friends, a job, and cheerleading responsibilities to show up for. One of the most recent times I'd seen him was when I was sixteen, when he and his wife had driven through my small town. They'd driven from Texas to Idaho with their two boys, Darek and Cory. They had not bothered to let me know that they were stopping at my grandparents. But when you're in high school and all you do is drag Main Street with your friends, it's hard to miss a brand-new, fancy forty-foot motorhome cruising through town.

I didn't really expect it to be him when my friends and I pulled up at the gas station to check out the fancy ride. Nor did I expect two new stepsisters to step out, dressed head-to-toe in new designer digs. It was a very awkward meeting at the gas station. I was crying so hard on the way home afterwards that I wrecked my car driving into a post in front of my house. How had he not thought it might be important to let me know he was adopting two grown girls and driving through my tiny hometown? He wasn't even going to tell me?

Thoughtfulness, clearly, was not his thing.

We made it to Coeur d' Alene with the U-Haul behind us, and I tried my best to settle in, but things were not quite right with my relationship with my bio dad. He would easily get angry at me for stupid stuff like asking him for money. He wanted to know if he was going to have to shell out cash to me forever. He would stare at me to the point where I was uncomfortable, often commenting on my weight or what I was wearing. He'd say that I was "too skinny" or that I'd "better watch" what I ate. Greg, who I still consider my dad, never ever noticed or talked about those kinds of things.

I started dating the star basketball player at the small community college I attended in North Idaho. He was a tall, beautiful black man named Dellondo Duvone Fox. How could you ever forget a name like that, or his funny, eccentric laugh and his sexy smile? My bio dad was not happy about this new relationship. He was an extremely prejudiced man who lived in Hayden Lake, Idaho. When I moved there, I was so naïve. I had no clue that the KKK had its headquarters there. My friend and I were once chased by two cars while driving around town after a basketball game. I was driving, and our two boyfriends were in the back—my girlfriend and I were in the front. Two cars with tinted windows approached on either side of us at the same time. It felt as if they were trying to run us off the road. You'd never seen such intense fear as the fear on our boyfriend's faces when we finally made it back to campus. Two black men, both over six feet tall, seriously sweating with anxiety in the middle of winter. Hayden Lake was a weird and racist small town. Those men were so out of place there, and I think that was one of the reasons I loved hanging out with them. I had never had black friends before. I don't even think we had any sort of brown people living in my tiny white-bread town. These guys were different than the other boys I'd known or dated, and I was very curious. I loved their unusually fun and playful banter. They were always cracking jokes and looking at life with a different perspective than most people I knew. After that incident, they never wanted to go to Hayden Lake again. I could hardly blame them. Although it was just on the outskirts of Coeur d'Alene, it definitely had a vibe of its own, and the people were all the same, like my bio dad, who was a kind of a redneck hick, himself. My dad was not in the KKK. However, he would often say things like "Why do you like hanging out with those niggers anyway?" These comments always sent shivers up my spine—they made me want to claw at his face. But I could only stare with the mean daggers of my eyes, hoping he got the message. I am sure this made me like Dellondo more. I found joy in being rebellious.

Dating or marrying someone from another race was frowned upon in my family. My mom had always threatened to disown me if I ever married a black man. "It wouldn't be fair to the children," she would say, trying to defend herself and her own ignorance.

I would often come home drunk after being out with Dellondo, pass out, and wake up to the smell of potatoes, whisky, and nastiness. My drunken biological father, after eating cold potatoes from the fridge, would come into my room. I would wake up—sometimes still half-drunk myself—to him trying to kiss me, his fingers in my pussy. I would scream and sob, both at the same time.

"What are you doing? Oh my God, what are you doing?"

I can still see my room and smell the potatoes laced with whiskey on his breath. Even the thought of baked potatoes, once a favorite of mine, makes me want to vomit. Whiskey, baked potatoes, a somewhat bloody steak, and several packs of cigarettes a day would sum up my father's diet—and smell. I still shiver with disgust thinking about those memories. I can vividly still see the dark wood paneling of the walls and the slatted closet doors, the big window to the front yard and the long driveway hidden amongst the tall pine trees. This vision, even now, instantly leaves me with disgust and the feeling of shame.

I am not certain how many times it happened. A few that I remember—but it could have been more. I tried hard to forget the devastating encounters that were shaping me into me.

Many years later, after coming home from the mental hospital the first time, I called my bio dad to confront him about the abuse. It was 2008. I woke up early, as I rarely slept and was always in a constant state of panic as my husband was threatening to take my children if I left him. I was surprised to catch my dad still asleep, since he always got up so early. I finally called him out on the incest. I cried, I screamed, and then I realized I had married a man who was so much like him, except that my husband didn't want to have sex with me. But my own biological father did? I felt so fucked up, a complete mess. I'd never had a great relationship with a man since my first couple of boyfriends, and yes, I did blame my father. I heard the sound of peeing as I talked to him. "What are you doing?" I screamed, "Oh my God, are you seriously touching your penis right now? Right now? While I am telling you how fucked up you have made me?" I screamed, and then I hung up.

Many years later when I talked with his wife, I told her what had happened. She wanted to know why I no longer wished to have a relationship with my father. "I do not want him around my daughters, or in their lives, period!" I said, and then told her what had happened. Apparently, later that day she tried talking to him, and they fought—physically fought—and he ended up breaking her jaw and landing himself in jail. She called later to let me know. Shortly after, he sent me a check for three thousand dollars, telling me never to contact him again. So, I didn't.

I felt good then about confronting him about the sexual abuse. I was trying to look at it, see my part in it, heal it, and let it go. There was nothing left of this relationship, nothing of interest to me, so I gladly cashed the check.

He recently sent me another check for my birthday, one hundred dollars. Now—ten years later? I mean, he paid me three grand to go away, then ten fucking years go by, and he feels a birthday card and a little meager cash will get me back? He had recently been calling, wanting to connect with me and possibly meet up. I needed much more than a hundred dollars and a birthday card to consider welcoming him back to my life. I felt like such a whore even cashing the check. I didn't want to take it, really. I carried it around for a couple of months, knowing that not cashing it would put him over the edge, keeping him from balancing his check book to the penny.

"No thank you, I have no interest in a relationship," I said, when I did finally take his call. He had wanted forgiveness—he had quit drinking. "Oh, I see," I said, "you need to cross me off your 12-step list? Listen," I told him, "I have forgiven you, but not for you, for me. Forgiveness is the gift you give to yourself." This saying was just one of my many little mantras that helped unburden me from my heavy backpack full of shit.

My dad was already a drunk when I was growing up, and probably started hitting the bottle even more after I confronted him the first time. While I was living with him, he'd start with a beer or two in the afternoon. Then came a "toddy," or possibly a few, consisting of whiskey and Coke. He sometimes got belligerent and mean when drinking heavily, screaming and yelling at all of us that he had to do everything around the house, including cooking and laundry. This wasn't entirely untrue. His wife, who was also aware of the weird energy, was also a drunk herself. She barely left the barstool, where she drank Diet Coke first thing in the morning, then adding in some whiskey later in the day. Often, her day would start with red beer (beer and tomato juice) and always cigarettes, which she'd puff on from morning until night, rarely leaving the kitchen. One time she checked herself into the mental hospital for shock treatments, as she just couldn't hack it. When she came home, she had forgotten that I even lived there, and she was certainly not up for hearing any of my problems. She was never quite the same after that trip to the looney bin.

While living with him, I, too, fell into drinking more and more, as well as binge eating and purging. Anything to block out the horrible transgressions that haunted my mind. I tried to brush the discomfort under the rug, as did my dad. But who could hide the elephant under the rug? Finally, I enrolled at the University of Idaho in Moscow—yes, the town, not the country, we used to always joke. I often wished I could move farther away. It wasn't nearly as far away as Russia, but even a few hours away would get me out of his house and into a sorority. This saved me for a whole year. But according to my dad, my grades were not up to par. Cs were not allowed, and my father put the kibosh on college. I would not be going back in the fall.

I tried to talk to him about the abusive encounters several times, but he would just say he was sorry. He didn't mean to; he said he loved me and that he'd also been violated as a child. This was not a good enough answer for me. It felt like an excuse. I had no plans to excuse him for these actions. I really hated him. I resented him and regretted that I had left my darling boyfriend behind for this new life with my abusive biological father. Now I knew I needed to get out of my dad's house, and soon.

He soon cut me off financially too, trying to control me just like my mother had. I felt stuck, and I was definitely not down for staying under his roof. So, I got a job working as a cocktail waitress at a local hangout—a Mexican restaurant with great food and a fun, laid-back vibe. I started at nineteen, which was the drinking age in Idaho back then. It was the eighties, and drinking, and soon even cocaine, became my thing. I'd often snort lines in the bathroom stall while working. "It's fine, even the owners are doing it!" my friend Fee Fee used to say, spooning tiny hits into my nostrils.

I then moved in with my latest boyfriend, Fred, but I caught him with another girl one night when I came home from work early. I almost broke down the door trying to get into our apartment. He wouldn't let me in, as he didn't want to deal with my hysteria. I was really pissed off as I walked downstairs and sat on the steps to cool off a bit. My neighbors were having a party, so I gratefully joined in, spending the night crying, while snorting heaps of cocaine and drinking endless amounts of vodka.

Fred was the bartender where I worked. This, too, was not a good situation. I needed to get control of my life. Staying at a friend's house after my three-day bender, I made the decision to get a job at Nordstrom. Hadn't I done an excellent job over the years going with my bio dad's wife to Nordstrom, helping her spend the allotted thousand dollars of cash that my dad so freely handed out? On occasion, she would offer to buy me a top, and then say, "Don't tell your dad, I don't want to get in trouble for spoiling you."

I snorted the last of my eighties cocaine and decided to quit this new-found habit cold turkey. I could hardly afford it, anyway, especially without the stupid boyfriend supplying it. The next day, I borrowed some random dress from the closet of the friend I was staying with, drove the thirty minutes to Spokane, and walked into Nordstrom, determined to walk out with a job.

6

THE ACCEPTABLE ADDICTION

1986

She was a spitfire. I liked her the minute I saw her on the Brass Plum floor, moving a giant round clothing rack across the floor. She was a teeny slip of a girl with long, white-blonde hair and big blue eyes. Her piercing determination and energy were overwhelming, and I liked it. I knew she must be in charge, so I walked right up, stuck out my hand, and said, "Hi, I'm Kami, I have wanted to work here my whole life, and I am here to apply for a job. Are you the manager of this department?" She gave me a quick nod and a once-over as she firmly shook my hand. Her name was Nicole. She led me into her tiny office and, after a brief interview, hired me on the spot. I would start the next day. I was beyond elated. Nothing had ever felt so right in my life—I was on my way.

Thus began my lifelong career in the clothing business. I showed up for my first day of work early and excited, determined to be the hardest worker. I vowed to do anything to move up the ranks. I was in heaven as I soon made friends with the big crew of girls. I was at the bottom of the food chain in this large pack of women. I tried hard to fit in and looked forward to getting promoted. I longed to feel the respect that

I would soon earn from my coworkers for a job well done. The promotion happened fairly quickly.

After only three months, I became the 97 girl, which meant I was in charge of the Brass Plum accessories. It was a job so tedious and exhausting that nobody but me really wanted to do it. I would spend hours making everything perfect, untangling countless necklaces and filling up the earring holders. I could almost count and colorize all the bright-colored socks in my head. Nicole, as my manager, would joke at my intense ownership over the accessories area. "Taking Ownership" was something Nordstrom promoted and rewarded, and I was all for it. It was only another two months before I became the assistant manager of Brass Plum. I arrived for work well before the security department. I learned to take the freight elevator up to the top floor at six a.m. every morning. I was thrilled about being the first in the store. It was like being a kid in a giant candy store. I loved the energy, the smell, and the vibe of the place. I was elated about my new life and the women I worked with. I rented a tiny apartment in Spokane just down the street from Nordstrom. It was a newly renovated early-1900s building, and I adored the old architecture that exuded such charming energy. Nicole even moved into the same building shortly after. We walked to work in our high-top reeboks and our short miniskirts, while carrying our high heels to change into before the store opened. I was settling in perfectly. After I worked for the company for only six months, Bill Nordstrom himself, the store manager, asked me at the ripe age of twenty-four to be the manager of the Brass Rail, the young men's department. I said no, I knew nothing of men's clothing or how to dress a guy. Besides, I totally loved my job at Brass Plum.

Bill came back the next day, asking, "What are you going to do about the section across the way?"

"The denim is perfect," I answered confidently, looking in the direction he was pointing. I had just redone it myself, stacking the jeans perfectly—merchandising had already become my thing.

"No, the other denim," he laughed, "the *men's* denim. I have seen your work ethic, Kami. The rest you can learn. Take the job. You will like the men's division better, anyway."

How could I not take his advice and the job he was offering? His name was on the door, after all, and, of course, he was right. I decided to take the job and threw myself into every aspect of it. Merchandising was my favorite! I loved moving things around and showcasing new items and making things look fresh. "Stacking them high and watching them fly," we always chimed. This was one of Nordstrom's many selling mantras.

I also learned all about the things I didn't really enjoy doing, like scheduling, budgeting, and inventory. I learned most of my management and people skills the hard way, making lots of mistakes and learning from them as quickly as I could. I had almost zero outside social life, albeit the weekend-only binge drinking with my new best friend, Nicoli Leonard, the nickname I gave to Nicole.

I spent the next year learning everything I could about the business, and I was ruthless about it. I even got one of my own bosses fired in my determination to take ownership and improve my business. It was a bold move, but I had Bill Nordstrom cheering me along, and I ate it up. I soon got promoted to Seattle, a big store in South Center Mall, and I was ecstatic. This was the big league. I increased my credit card limit and bought the "get promoted" suits and a million pairs—or so it seemed—of Donna Karan hosiery, and a new pair of black pumps. I was ready to "drink the Kool-Aid," as we called it, which meant you learned to conform, say, and do all the right things in order to get promoted, and I was not only willing to drink it, but serve it up too. I was all in.

I rented a small apartment that I rarely used in the darling community of Green Lake and lived with roommates that I never saw. I really only slept and showered there, as work was more than a full-time focus. What little social life I did have all came from work. For the next three years, I worked six days a week, ten-plus hours a day, and never thought anything of it or the family I had left behind. Work consumed me. I managed a big sales team and cultivated some of the top salespeople in the company. I was consumed with work and spent every penny dressing for the part. My uniform usually consisted of short black skirts, black opaque hosiery, and, of course, the pumps. It was the eighties—I had big curly hair and wore blazers, silk tanks, and suits with big shoulder pads. I drove a white Honda CRX with a hatchback, perfect to throw my skis into and drive to the local mountain, but I didn't love the skiing there, or maybe I just didn't take enough time to enjoy much about life. I just wanted to work. My determination and drive to do a great job consumed my time and all of my energy. I didn't even date much then, and the relationships I did have were all like one train wreck after another. And I had a few, at least, one-night stands one after another. I was not the same person as before, but I wasn't sure who I was really. I may have worn the blazer with the big shoulders and the perfect black pumps, but I still had a hard time stepping into my own shoes. It was nice for a while, conforming and pleasing, having the feeling that I was winning. I cared more about being applauded at the monthly award meetings in front of my peers than anything else—called up and given a proper, hard handshake from one of the Nords (Nordstrom family member) or someone else of importance. It was embarrassing and thrilling at the same time. We would all stand up in front of everyone, in our best black suits, ready to receive what was called cash call. It was a small token of cash; I don't even remember how much it was. It was never about the money anyway. It was about the accolades and acknowledgment of a job well done. I loved the feeling afterwards as you walked onto the sales floor, lipstick reapplied, perfect pumps clicking just so, head held high as friends and colleagues continued to congratulate you throughout the day.

I quickly learned it was easy to win if you had a strong team, and I loved the challenge and the reward of cultivating the best people I could. I hired a new assistant manager named Ray, and we soon became fast friends. We were more like a family; we spent so much time together. Ray was a beautiful man—Persian, with gorgeous black hair, piercing blue eyes and amazing skin. He was an impeccable dresser and had a smile that would light up any room. His bubbling, champagne-like demeanor was so infectious, people just swarmed to him to drink it up. Gorgeous on the inside and out, he approached everything with his big, open heart. He could talk the salespeople into doing almost anything he asked, all while still selling their asses off. He was smooth like that, and always kept every situation under control. We learned so much from one another, often contemplating life and challenging one another's growth while folding endless heaps of Stüssy T-shirts together. Sometimes we laughed until we cried, and we were always brainstorming ideas about how to improve business, as work was what made us tick. We enjoyed the hard work and the acknowledgment we received; however, I knew it wouldn't last. I often teased him that our time together would be short-lived. He fit the Nordstrom mold perfectly, and I knew he would soon be promoted. Indeed, he was offered the first manager job for Façonnable, an exclusive, high-end brand from Nice opening in the Nordstrom in downtown Seattle. It was an honor, as this was the new crown jewel of the men's division. It was perfect for him. I enjoyed seeing him so dapper and happy in his new element of perfectly pressed and folded high-end designer men's shirts, ties, and sportswear. I loved catching him working so hard behind the counter, all while exuding such grace and goodness.

I, too, got promoted, but not exactly to the dream job I had anticipated.

7
NORTH TO ALASKA

1989

Alaska was probably last on the list of places I wanted to live, and it was definitely not a place I longed to work. I had grown up in Utah and had been living in the Northwest, but Alaska? Okay, yeah, all the beautiful men and all. I often joked later that I met all two of the beautiful men and that, yes, I dated them both! I had wanted to climb the ladder, so I should have been ecstatic about being offered a buying job at Nordstrom. The volume was the same as in the department I had managed in Seattle, and I would be the buyer of only one store, but I would also be part of a seasoned buying team. I should've been thrilled. I was only twenty-four and being offered a buying job. But I wasn't very happy about it. After going back and forth a few times, I finally accepted. I bought a bright yellow Jeep Wrangler and caught a flight to Alaska just four days later. The movers would come and pack up my life from the quaint community in Green Lake. I'd hardly taken the time to enjoy the town, so there would be nothing to miss. Work was at the forefront of my life. The move to Anchorage would be a simple transition. Stafford, one of my friends, had moved to Alaska from Seattle the year before to be the men's sportswear buyer, and he needed a roommate. He had a great apartment just a few minutes from Nordstrom. It was a 1970s condo with a giant picture window that looked out onto the inlet. It was a groovy place, close to work and not far from the endless coastal trails that wrapped around the town of Anchorage.

"It's going to be a great adventure," I kept saying, still trying to convince myself.

I stayed at a nearby hotel until my belongings and new Jeep arrived, then moved in with Stafford, who, like his apartment, was pretty groovy. We hosted several themed parties, with hip music, signature cocktails, and fun snacks. Stafford was always up for fun and entertainment—good times were always on the agenda.

I had only been in Alaska a year or so when I woke up one night in a sweat of panic. Something was wrong. I couldn't sleep and an odd feeling had come over me. The next morning, I got a call from a friend letting me know that Ray, my beautiful Persian friend, had been shot and killed the night before while defending his girlfriend at a night club.

Of course, I was devastated and could hardly eat or sleep, as Ray was all I could think about. I kept having this odd feeling that his presence was with me, that he was not at peace, and that he was somehow estranged. Ray was an extremely gentle being, and his being taken in such a violent way shook me. His presence would not go away. I asked around for help, and someone suggested I see a local shaman for some guidance.

She didn't seem like a shaman, but I had never met one, so how would I know? We sat for quite some time while I listened as she revealed aspects of my life and my connection with Ray. Once she realized he had passed, she explained to me that he was stuck between the dimensions because he had been taken so suddenly by being violently shot in the neck. She gathered a few things for me and gave me some tips on how to conduct a ritual to help with his transition.

Because Ray and I had been so closely connected, and because I was an "open channel" (whatever that meant), he came to me after his passing. She said I needed to help him cross over. She told me I would be traveling soon, which I was—to Seattle—and that I would soon go back to where he had passed and do certain rituals. These prayers would help guide him to where he needed to go. She also told me that the "1111 window," in particular, would be a guiding light for me: these numbers would be significant to my spiritual journey. They would show up to help me understand the energetic vibrations of the universe. I left with a small satchel of items for the ritual, feeling a bit dazed. I had no idea of the journey this little magic pouch and I were about to embark on.

The first ritual took place in downtown Seattle, where Ray had left his body. I placed the flowers, dried herbs from the pouch, and a crystal on the sidewalk across the street from where he'd passed. I also lit a candle and recited the prayers I had written, along with a small story I'd written about looking for the light and beauty. I felt Ray's presence and told him, "You are safe, I am here for you, I love you." I told him that he had charmed my life so much, with his jaunty demeanor and deep blue eyes that spoke volumes, but most of all with his giant, pure heart. I sat with his energy in quiet meditation until I felt his presence gently leave me. I left downtown with such a sense of peace, of meaning, of life, and of more questions that I longed to explore.

Back home in downtown Anchorage, I moved into a little apartment above a bookstore. Stafford had recently moved back to Seattle. Over the next year, I spent countless hours reading every shamanic and spiritual book I could get my hands on. My work was on autopilot. I was once again cultivating the best people to work with, so my small business as the young men's department buyer and manager almost ran itself. I continued to be ahead of trend, and I won monthly achievement awards, but my new passion was on spiritual studies and being outdoors.

I snow skied in the winter months, often going by myself. I prided myself for living in Alaska and for being a badass. I was unafraid of the great outdoors. Although I was kind of a girly-girl, I enjoyed every minute I was out in nature. I had started skiing at age ten and loved being in the mountains. I also started hiking, mountain biking, and rollerblading on the endless trails. Anything to be outside in the majestic beauty of Alaska. I had never in my life felt more connected to Mother Nature than I did in the three years of living in Alaska, and she never failed to surprise me with her unending display of natural beauty or disappoint me with her inhabitants.

Once, while riding my bike on a nearby trail, I came around the corner, and there he was—a giant moose. I slammed on my brakes, but being the rookie that I was, I flew right over the handlebars and landed smack on my back in front of the moose. He looked at me for the dork that I was and then casually sauntered off. My friend Lizzie shot around the corner behind me to see me looking like a yard sale, my things strewn all over the trail. We laughed so hard while we tried not to pee our pants!

It was always fun and adventure with my Alaska posse. Alaska is a place where—once you live there—you have to defend it in every conversation. The fact that you've lived in Alaska, alone, makes you an interesting person. We enjoyed it to its fullest, partying under the Northern Lights as they danced through the sky. We jumped from the rooftop of my friend's house into the snowdrifts while having an outdoor bonfire in minus-zero-degree temperatures on New Year's Eve, then I slept in a tent outdoors with my darling Alaska boyfriend, Butch. We fished and hiked. I was certainly making the best of things.

I was having a great time studying spirituality, traveling, and hanging out with all my Alaskan friends, but I was also getting the three-year itch to move on to the next thing. Business was down trending in retail. Grunge becoming the new "in" thing meant people were now shopping in thrift stores. I had recently been passed over for a couple of promotions, which took its toll on my confidence. I was ready to move, and somewhere warm would certainly be nice.

A friend of mine was the company's San Diego buyer, and she needed a department manager for her Escondido store. "I'll take it," I said one night at dinner when I met her on one of our many buying trips to Seattle.

"It's a step down. Why do you want it?" asked my friend.

"Um, hello! I have lived in Alaska for three years. I have frozen my ass off and been turned down for the last three promotions because nobody wants to pay for me to move, and San Diego sounds truly delightful right now!" I said.

A few days later, back in Alaska, I got a call from Dan Nord, Bill's brother. He was currently one of the store managers in San Diego. We had worked next to one another in Seattle when he was the shoe buyer. Our departments had been side by side, and we soon became buddies. He was cool and easygoing. I'd often redone all his displays when my OCD tendencies made me push over from my own department to his. He always thanked me and never seemed to mind my creative takeover.

"Kami, you're still up there?" he asked.

"Yes, Dan, get me out of here!" I laughed, trying hard not to cry at the same time.

We talked for a few minutes, catching up. He then thanked me for my hard work and dedication and said he would put in a call for me to the other store manager. He hung up saying he really hoped that I would get the job, as I had really shown my loyalty. I really hoped so too, and that the company would pay for my move. He was true to his word, and the move was paid for. I was soon driving my jeep down the coast from Seattle to sunny San Diego, with its endless beaches and palm trees.

I would be fine. I soon met a new bunch of girls and two new best friends, Jodi and Kiley, who also worked with me at Nordstrom in Escondido. After only three months, Leslie, my friend and boss, got promoted to corporate Merchandise Manager, and I got her job, buying for the four San Diego stores. I had done it—I had landed my new dream job. I was beyond thrilled. It was so much fun buying and traveling—mostly to Seattle and all over California. Meeting new people and going to cool parties, all with a seasoned buying team to learn from, equaled nonstop fun for me. Working in the young men's division, I worked with up-and-coming brands such as Mossimo, Billabong, Quiksilver, Stüssy, Rusty, and Lucky Brand. I was not from the beach, but I loved the beach lifestyle and surf culture, and I embraced the fun that came along with it. That's not to say it wasn't hard work—it was. The stress from running part of a multimillion-dollar business was never-ending. Managing people, answering to upper management, and working with many vendors, all while juggling all the other balls in the air, kept a girl quite busy. But I was on top of the world for three more years.

I loved my work, but I could also hear my biological clock ticking. I would be pushing thirty soon, and I longed for children and a family—and for romantic love with someone I felt a true connection with. I wanted the fun and family that I was experiencing at work be more than work. I wanted it to be a constant in my life. I wanted a close-knit family—I rarely talked to anyone from my own family, certainly not with any of my parents, and I longed to create a family of my own.

I used to laugh and say to my friends that "The first man with a ring wins!" My words would be prophetic. My three-year itch, as I called it, had me open to new connections and possibilities.

I was ready.

8

LIVING THE CALIFORNIA DREAM

I was on my way home to San Diego from one of my many buying trips to Seattle when I saw him. I had arrived at the airport early and had planned to do a little paperwork. He caught my attention right away as he pretended to read the newspaper. He was wearing sunglasses, which were pulled down, and we immediately caught eyes. He was tan and handsome with a stern face and smiley blue eyes. He had a cool-guy attitude, yet he was quiet, approachable, and intriguing.

I walked right up and sat down in the empty seat beside him. I pulled out the endless stack of paperwork that went along with buying in those days, pre-computer. We made small talk, and he said his name was Dave. We kept looking at one another, clearly finding each other interesting. He was also from San Diego. We laughed that we were on the same flight and not sitting very close to our gate. We talked for a while and then walked to the gate and boarded the plane together. Why hadn't I taken a little extra time to do my makeup? I always hated doing my makeup. Tired from a week of product development meetings at Nordstrom, I'd taken a break from the need to look and dress perfectly. I stopped just off the plane at the restroom to check myself before going to pick up my bag from baggage claim. I gave myself an up-and-down check in the mirror—jeans, boots, black blazer, white T-shirt, curly natural hair. At age twenty-nine, I was still cute, but I already felt old. I put on some lipstick, gave my hair a fluff, and smiled at myself for some extra confidence. He was waiting at the baggage claim, staring back at me with that smiley smirk I would soon come to know and love. I walked up next to him and smiled back as he asked for my number. I gave my standard answer, "I don't give out my number, but I'll take yours." I realize now that I was such a control freak, needing to guard my emotions at all times.

I waited a week and then called him. We agreed to meet at George's at the Cove, in La Jolla, for drinks. I was nervous and excited, but as soon as I walked in and saw his sparkly blue eyes and gave him a hug I was at ease. He was wearing a crisply ironed blue shirt tucked into his tight jeans and, again, I thought he was pretty cute. We had drinks, snacks, and a blueberry bread pudding that was to die for. Not only was he handsome, but he was also secure and respectful. After our third or fourth date, I barely went home, and I left my perfect party life behind in Pacific Beach. At the time, I lived just a few houses away from the beach in what my friends and I fondly called the "pink palace," a four-bedroom pink house with a rooftop panoramic view of the ocean and a big jacuzzi. I had such great friends, and I loved my life. In fact, life was close to perfect in my mind. My friends and I roller-bladed around the bay after work. We met at the beach every Sunday and then went back to my house for margaritas and a sunset jacuzzi. This was usually followed by a visit to one of our favorite local pubs for a little dinner, pool playing, and drinks. And now that I had just met a great guy, life was getting better every day.

On just our third date, we talked of marriage and agreed to start a relationship. A few months later, he helped me pack up and move out of my beach house to shack up with him. Single life had been fine, but my workaholic lifestyle and late-night partying habits hadn't meshed well together. I really wanted to settle down and have a family of my own. I would be thirty in a year, and I was a bit behind on the "life plans" that I had set for myself. Thirty felt so old to start a family compared to my friends back home in Utah. I had already come such a long way from the day I ran away from home many years ago.

I said goodbye to my roommates, the two Daves. "My" Dave packed me up and moved me to Encinitas. It was not even thirty miles away, but it may as well have been three hundred. My life and connections in the small beach community I'd been living in were never quite the same. It was fine—life was moving fast and in the right direction. Once again, as always, I welcomed the change. It wasn't long before he popped the question. We were on the beach at sunset with a small bonfire and a bottle of Jordon champagne. He gathered driftwood and crafted a heart around me, and he got on one knee. We both cried—he really was so sweet.

Dave was so perfect for me—and I wanted children. My biological clock was starting to get the best of me. I'd always thought I'd get married and have children—it is what you are taught from the very beginning growing up in Utah. It's engrained in the Mormon culture: "Go forth and replenish the earth!" Mormons take this very literally. I certainly had no plans to help replenish the earth, but a couple of kids would be great.

As of late, I've heard many rumors flying around that "they," who are currently running the world, also have plans in place for the exact opposite.

The downsizing of the population of the Earth.

9

EVERYTHING NEW

I was about to get married!

My soon-to-be husband's father was not well. He struggled with Alzheimer's. Dave's mom did not want to attend a big wedding, so we decided to skip having one. We had gotten to this point fairly independently and decided we could get married without our parents being present. We decided on Jamaica. Those who wanted to attend would make the journey, and those that didn't wouldn't. I believe my mother was relieved, since she was afraid to fly and always complained of not having enough money. I think she was quite happy not to come. My bio dad and his wife decided to come, which was probably why my stepdad and his wife decided to bow out.

We hadn't even received our bags when the bellman showed up with the biggest marijuana buds I had ever seen. I was angry with Dave that marijuana was the first thing he was concerned about, but marijuana was his thing. He had started smoking daily when he was thirteen and had rarely ever stopped. He spent the week stoned, and I spent the week fairly pissed off. Had it not been for one of my best friends, Jodi, who showed up and surprised me before the wedding, the whole thing could have been a disaster.

Right before we were about to be married, a giant torrential downpour came roaring through the island. I wasn't quite sure how to get from point A to point B, both of which were outside bungalows, in the pouring rain in a wedding dress. The rain was coming down in sideways sheets of brutal wrath. I ran to the front desk crying, barefoot and soaked in my bikini, feeling like a drowned rat. I hardly looked like a pampered bride about to be married. They offered to give me a room to get dressed in that was close to the new ceremony location—which was a small inside restaurant that happened to be closed on this particular day. I needed to hurry though, as we would have to keep our time commitment with the small group of people we'd hired to officiate our tiny wedding. I had less than an hour to shower and get ready for my wedding. I packed up my dress and essentials and ran to the new room to get myself together. I had no makeup artist, no hairstylist, and nobody to do my nails or help with my dress. Not only that, which was not a big deal to me, but I was beyond horrified when my bio dad showed up at my door, expectantly planning to walk me down the wet sidewalk to the place I would soon be married.

This was not what I had planned. I wanted to walk by myself. I had gotten this far in life all alone. What had he done for me? He'd offered up a few grand towards the trip, but I hadn't even really seen him in a few years. He and his current wife were having the trip of a lifetime, drinking all day long and going on all of the adventures I wished I could afford. Now here he stood, my father, with an ugly denim shirt adorned with a too-short pink polyester tie and tie clip. He wore khaki pants and white tennis shoes. The pink polyester tie matched perfectly with the pink hair scrunchy that held his wife's curly waves back into a ponytail. She was dressed in a pink dress and flip flops. How was this my wedding party? It was a far cry from any storybook wedding I had envisioned for myself, and vision was never something I had lacked.

Apparently, I didn't understand that vision for myself, for it would be a while yet.

I swallowed hard, trying not to sob. God help me, I thought, as I looked around at the stacked-up tables and chairs on one side of the wall, stacked boxes on the other. Furniture and whatnot had been brought in to keep them out of the rain. Miscellaneous items were strewn about—umbrellas, boxes, and other stuff. Being the visual beauty whore that I am, I quietly cried for myself as I stood amongst the crap and married this man.

At the end of the short ceremony, the tiny three-piece band played some Jamaican tunes, and then, just like that, the rain stopped. The clouds parted and the sun came out to shine— gone were the footprints in the sand, gone were the clouds. The blue and pink skies came out to say hello and bless us, the sky cracked open, and it was absolutely gorgeous, the sun shining brightly on our newly wedded faces. I tried to assure myself that this was a sign, that everything would be okay.

Later that night, I thought I was so cute, and even sexy, as I jumped on the bed wearing my veil and pretty cream lace lingerie. He seemed to barely notice me, or he was too stoned to even consummate our marriage on our wedding night. This was crushing to me and certainly a bad omen, I thought. Why didn't he want to have sex with me? I already knew he didn't like kissing—he was very open about that. I had already decided to settle without much kissing. Had that been a mistake?

Dave and I spent the rest of the trip relaxing and soaking up the sun, and we took a day trip on a little dingy to a tiny, desolate island. Dave paid the guy to drop us off and come back and pick us up later in the afternoon. We packed some drinks and snacks and spent the afternoon alone exploring and making love on the beach. That day was one of the best days we would ever spend together.

Life was going to be just fine, I told myself.

Besides, I had an exciting new job to return to. Before leaving on our trip, I had been offered a new job as the women's sales manager for Rusty, one of my top-selling brands. It would be a new challenge, and I was over the moon about it. At Nordstrom, I had the opportunity of working with some fantastic people and top brands. But somehow, I knew Nordstrom wouldn't be my long-term home. I had been there ten years, and it felt like a good run. I found the Nordstrom culture to be conservative, and that I was certainly not. Nordstrom was growing like crazy and centralizing most of the buying teams in Seattle. I had already lived there once, in my early career, and I had no plans of going back. I loved the Southern California beach lifestyle. Rusty Surf apparel was up-and-coming and soon to be my number one brand at Nordstrom. I found that I loved the surf industry, and I made great connections with most of the owners of these big brands. Women's surfing was just starting to boom. Roxy, the Quiksilver-owned women's line, was starting to get some traction. I saw this trend coming and I wanted in. I pitched the idea to Rusty, who internally had been talking of launching a new women's division. They offered me a position to start up this new women's brand, and I would begin as soon as I returned from my honeymoon. Dave was very supportive and patient with me. I wouldn't have been able to make this change without him cheering me along or supporting me financially until my commission checks started kicking in.

It would be a small team to launch the women's division: me, a designer, and soon one marketing person. But I was ecstatic. I sold my tiny convertible Miata and bought the "freeway floater," a Honda Accord grown-up car, for the hour-each-way commute to Irvine.

I was beside myself in gratitude. New job, new life, new theme car. They always went together for me. I was soon traveling the country, making twice as much money as I had at Nordstrom and sharing office space with one of the most amazing women I had ever met. She had a celestial name—I called her my "Celestial Friend," and we became fast friends. We would spend the next three years doing almost everything together. Life was grand.

10

RIDING THE GOOD WAVE

FALL 1996

I was definitely in the "green room," known to surfers as the sweet spot, barreled in a perfect wave of the good life. My new job working in the surf industry was on fire, and I was enjoying every minute of it, traveling, commuting, and also making some pretty sweet cash. I loved planning the line for the next season, predicting what would sell and how much of each style, and I was pretty good at it. I found pride in the bottom line and kept a tight inventory. It was stressful and challenging, growing a new business, but I had a knack at knowing what to buy—what to develop and how much—making our division very profitable. I loved the creativity and the game of the numbers, and I was helping to create a multimillion-dollar brand in just a few short years. I was proud.

I felt accomplished, but, of course, I also wanted a baby. After all, having my own family was really all I had ever wanted. I wanted to feel like I belonged. I was on-top-of-the-world happy—why not make it even better?

I was in downtown San Francisco with my best friend, Jodi, the day I found out I was pregnant. We had flown to the city for a weekend of shopping and fun. I had been feeling nauseous and couldn't eat my sushi and could hardly drink my beer the night before at dinner, which was not typical. I woke up early, left the hotel, and walked to a drug store to buy a pregnancy test. I hurried back to the hotel to find out if this was the reason for my sickness. Yep! Preggers!

"Jodi, wake up, wake up! I'm pregnant," I screamed, as I jumped on her bed with my test while calling my husband to share the news.

He, too, was ecstatic as he yelled out to his office at work, "We're pregnant!"

Which made me laugh as I said, "Well, I think I am the pregnant one!"

He told me to buy something fun for myself and that he looked forward to picking me up at the airport. Jodi and I shopped all day and talked about my being pregnant. I was certain I was having a girl—I just knew it. I bought a darling gold-lined antique teacup and saucer for my baby-to-be, and we shopped, laughed, and planned my baby shower. I was thrilled, nervous, and excited about being a mom.

"What, a boy, I'm having a boy?" I said to the technician when I went to my first ultrasound. I was so surprised. I was sad, but I soon adjusted. I just wanted a baby, regardless of the sex, and I really could not wait. My pregnancy went fairly smoothly—I ate boxes and boxes of Apple Jacks cereal, something I never ate. Rarely did I eat the perfectly packaged poison that most grocery stores are stocked full of. It was so funny to me, and I wondered just what this kid would be like. Would he be sugary and sweet like the cereal I couldn't get enough of? I had two baby showers, one with my friends and one at work. Both parties were for "Max." I painted his beach-themed bedroom blue and filled out the announcements. Three weeks after my due date, I went in to see when "he" was coming.

"You're having a girl, you know, that right?" said this technician the day before Samantha was born. I had gotten used to the idea of having a boy—it seemed all boys loved and adored their mothers, and I longed for that—but all along I had known she was a girl. For months, I had been mourning the girl I thought I was carrying and had begun to embrace the new boy energy. I wasn't wrong about the strong energy—this girl was going to be a firecracker, and she would certainly run her own show, but I just had no idea how big this show was going to be. At this point, boy or girl, I just wanted to be done with this pregnancy. My head was whirling, my body fat, hands and feet swollen. I was ready.

After two days of labor and a C-section, Samantha Jolene was born. I didn't get to hold her or see her though, as she was whisked away to neonatal intensive care with fluid in her lungs. This is where it began—the overwhelming fear of losing her. My pain was already so deep, and I had only been a mother a few minutes. I was so scared and nervous that she would not be okay that I immediately started to cry. I was sure that she had felt my anxiety the minute we met. I was a nervous wreck. My best friends—Jodi, "Dodo," and Kiley, "Kiley Boo," (the nicknames that would come later from this child of mine), showed up with boxes full of girl baby clothes, as everything I had prepared was for a boy. They brushed my hair, put a little makeup on me, and tried to put me back together a bit while Dave followed Samantha to the neonatal intensive care unit.

Samantha was a daddy's girl from day one. At eight pounds, seven ounces, she looked more like a toddler than a newborn next to the premature little babes in the NICU. I asked Dave to go with her, to watch over her. I didn't even get to hold her. This was probably where the heartbreak and disconnect started for both of us. That initial bonding is so important. Dave was the first to hold her, first to nurture her, and first to pick her up and connect with her. The NICU was on a different floor, and I had just had a C-section. It was hard to spend much time with her since I had to pump and bottle-feed those first few days. Nursing and connecting did not come easy for me. I felt scared and alone.

After several days in intensive care, we were sent home. Dave didn't take time off work, and, of course, my friends were all working, and besides, it wasn't their job to help me. But that's what I needed—I needed some help. I was in so much pain lifting the baby when I wasn't supposed to after surgery. But what choice did I have? She needed me, and I was so overwhelmed and fearful that I wasn't doing everything right. Where was my mother when I needed her? How could someone miss their grandchild being born, anyway?

But she was rarely around then, well not for me anyway. When I was a child, she usually showed up with gifts—guilt gifts were what they felt like. When she was mad at me, she would threaten, "I hope you have a daughter just like you, one that breaks your heart," like I had hers. Could this fussy, darling little baby, with strawberry blonde hair and big blue eyes—so sweet, innocent, and perfect—possibly grow up to break my heart?

My mother was a much bigger witch than me, I thought now. Her curse probably would indeed be true, I thought as I dialed her number, trying hard not to cry.

"I need help. Please can you come?" I told her of the challenging time I was having, exhausted and not sleeping. I was having a hard time just going up and down the stairs with the baby from my bedroom, which I was not supposed to do. I then offered to pay for her ticket to come to San Diego to help.

"Please," I begged, "I am not doing a good job with this whole motherhood thing. Please can you come? I am a mess!"

She couldn't come.

She was too busy getting ready for my younger sister's wedding. The wedding was planned, and I was expected to get on a plane to Utah with my newborn baby, who had just been released from intensive care. I wasn't sure how I would get through the next two hours, let alone get on a plane with Dave and Sam in less than two weeks.

I was hysterical and crying. "What? What are you trying to say to me?" I asked her again, not understanding what she was saying.

Now she, too, was crying.

"And don't let your new baby around your father!" she said, out of nowhere.

"What?" I said again, still not processing what she'd said. "What? What the fuck are you trying to say?" I screamed back at her. Then she began screaming and crying hysterically. For once, just this once, I thought this was my turn to be hysterical. Nope, not with my mother. She had to make everything about her, always.

She had missed the birth of her grandchild, and there I was, reaching out, practically begging her for help, and she was trying to tell me that my dad, not my biological father but the man who had raised me my entire life, was a child molester? Even worse, she was insinuating that he molested babies?

I couldn't hear this. I racked my brain, mentally backtracking over my childhood years. I felt as if she would do or say just about anything to keep love from coming my way. She was a wreck, and she matched my hysteria with her own. I hung up.

Dave, Sam, and I attended my sister's wedding, staying in a nearby motel. For once, my mother didn't ask us to stay with her. She was just too busy, she said. She had too many things going on with a fairly full house of her best friends already. There would be no nurturing for me or even my newborn baby. My mom had chosen her friends to be near her, not me. I silently cried for myself and my new child while looking at the motel's cheap décor—ugly floral bedspread, the beat-up laminated wood dresser, and the worn and stained carpet, and me with my bad attitude. The wedding was beautiful, and my sister, Keri, made an absolutely stunning bride. I loved seeing her so happy. However, as usual, I couldn't wait to get back to my life, away from Utah, and away from my mother.

Dave, of course, was incredible and great with Sam. They already had a bond that I was secretly jealous of. As soon as we flew home, I hired a full-time nanny. I couldn't wait to get back to work at Rusty. I wanted to do what I was good at in a place where I felt in control of my life. I even planned and attended a national sales meeting in Mexico, leaving Samantha at home with her dad and nanny. She wasn't even two months old, and I left her.

Maybe I wasn't a better mother than my own.

Family life seemed perfect for a while until I became jealous of the nanny, who got to spend all day with Sam. I started to feel like I was really missing out on her life, and it started to get the best of me. I felt the urge to be home with her. I just needed to figure out how. I added up all the money we spent on the nanny, the gas, the cute clothes, the travel, and the taxes. We were in a very high tax bracket with our double incomes. Why work so hard, I thought, when I could stay home with my baby? I crunched the numbers and talked my husband into letting me stay home. Just the money we saved in taxes alone was more than most people made in a year. We had moved into a newly built house and had a small, manageable mortgage. Thanks to my big paychecks, we had paid for many of the building costs along the way. But I wanted to raise my daughter myself. My current job had kept me way too busy and away from home, and I didn't want to miss out on anything. Dave was a very involved parent, and he and Sam had a very strong bond. I wanted this bond too, and he agreed. I got our finances all in order—we were pretty set. Dave's work as a building inspector was getting busier, and he agreed to let me stay home and be a full-time mom, something I felt was very important. I loved waking up with Sam, planning our day—what we would do, who we might see, and all the fun we would have. The small stuff, I realized, was important.

I had always loved working, but this new challenge of being a good parent was what was most important. I thought nothing of giving up the job that I had worked for my entire life, even at the height of my career. I just didn't care. I wanted so badly to have the mother-daughter bond that I had always longed for.

I was soon in my new heaven—I joined a playgroup of moms with babies the same age, and I was pregnant with baby number two. This time I would wait and find out the gender. I was so content having my own family. I was truly in my bliss.

The second I saw the little rose bud I was in love—Savannah Rose, "Savvy," we called her. She was born on 2/2/2000. She was such a love, just like her birth numerology numbers, which easily added up to six, meaning love. Six was the Lovers card in the tarot. We called her Rose, because that's what the nurse said when she saw her: "Look at this little rosebud!" I had wanted to name her after my grandmas, both of whom were named Georgia. My husband would not concede, so I decided on Savannah, since that was the closest thing I could think of to Georgia.

I had to have a C-section, however. I had even hired a midwife who would encourage the natural birth and help me through it, but it wasn't going to happen. The on-call doctor who came to check on me asked if I could wait until the next morning to deliver. He had to leave the hospital by 6:00 p.m.

"Oh, hell no, I am not waiting another night. You'd better hurry up if you need to leave by six!" I said.

It was only a couple of hours away. Savannah Rose was delivered at 6:24 p.m. on Groundhog Day. We had an instant bond. It helped that there were no complications—no panic or stress. This time, bringing home a new baby, I knew what to expect. I wasn't afraid, I was calm and so content. I could just sit with my baby and watch Sam play—the house could be in chaos, and for once I just enjoyed myself.

Savvy was easy, which was a relief, because her sister, now two, challenged everything. She had to be held down to even have her teeth brushed, until she would finally do it herself. Sam never wanted a babysitter, and at preschool she was a bit defiant and didn't like to be told what to do. We always joked that Sam often chose "the hard way." She was strong-willed, confident, and more than anything else, she was a daddy's girl.

Nonetheless, I was happy being home with them. We soon had season passes not only to Sea World and the Zoo, but also to the Wild Animal Park and Legoland. We lived a block from the beach, so my children pretty much grew up living a vacation life, and a good life it certainly was. Parks and playdates, kid parties, and moms' nights out for me. I loved being with my children and watching them experience life so innocently, as only children could do.

It was a dream life, and I got to live it. For a little while, anyway.

11

DIAGNOSED

The dream life came to a quick halt the year Samantha fell ill. Sam was only five at the time and wasn't feeling well. I had taken her to the doctor several times. I'd even had her back x-rayed, as she couldn't walk down the stairs and she seemed to be in so much pain. The last quack we'd seen said that she probably had anxiety and was acting out because I was going to be out of town for a few days. I wasn't sure where he'd gotten his medical degree, but yes, I was planning to go to Florida for the weekend for a trade show. I was going to help Angie, my childhood best friend, with her spa products. It would be like working again, but only for two days. I needed a small break from the pressures of full-time parenting. As any mother will tell you, full-time motherhood is no easy task. It would only be a couple of days, I kept reminding myself. I was already feeling guilty, and I hadn't even left yet. I went on the trip, then called that night to check in and say goodnight at the kids' bedtime. My neighbor answered the landline. The hair on the back of my neck immediately stood straight up as he said hello. Something was wrong—why was he answering my phone?

"What the fuck is going on?" I screamed into the phone, not even saying hello.

"You should call your husband, he is in the car," he said.

I hung up and called Dave.

He answered, his voice firm but hollow, "Hi. I am on the way to Children's Hospital with Sam; she was just diagnosed with leukemia."

"Leukemia?" I said out loud, looking over at Angie as she popped a sleeping pill. I dropped to the floor.

No wonder I'd had to be so far, far away, from home. It would certainly take the entire span of the country to thread together the newfound crack in my heart. If God and I ever really talked, we talked that night. I barely pulled myself together to get a cab to the airport that night, leaving behind most of my things and my snoring friend.

At the Jacksonville airport, I couldn't get a flight out until morning, and I didn't know what to do with myself, who to call, or what to do. My baby was clear across the fucking country and needed me. I walked through the airport and looked up to see a small sign for a chapel. It was curious—I had never seen a chapel in an airport before. I walked in, grateful to find solace in the small, reverent space. I prayed like I never prayed in my life before or since. I prayed until I was certain every giant god, goddess, and every single little fucking fairy nymph had heard me. I got up from the floor, where I had been sitting for what felt like endless hours in a cross-legged position with my back super straight and head slightly bowed. I prayed with the deepest respect of my being. As I got up, planning to leave, I noticed a tiny thank-you card on the little side table nestled next to the small green sofa. I picked it up, shaking my head in almost utter disbelief as I read:

"Thank you for this beautiful space, so perfect in this time of need.

Love,

Jolene"

I cried even more, if that is even possible, as I returned the tiny card to its place and sat back down on the floor. Now my prayers were those of the utmost gratitude. I knew God had heard me. He would answer my prayers. I don't know many Jolenes, but I had named my daughter Samantha Jolene after my aunt for a reason. She was, and still is, one of the strongest women I have ever met. At last count, my aunt had taken in and helped raise forty or more children. This little card was certainly a sign that my child, too, would be okay. I lifted my head, shifting my shoulders down and back, mentally plugging myself in like a battery, as I'd always thought best in order to utilize the body's energy to connect—to plug into the perfection of Mother Earth. I sat quietly in my intense meditation for the rest of the night, until the early morning, thanking the universe for this small sign, the acknowledgement of my prayers. I left the sweet little chapel with the deepest of knowing that I had been heard.

I continued my prayers quietly to myself as I boarded the plane. I don't remember the flight home; I only remember telling myself, "I've got this, I've got this. I've got this. No, God has this." I had no choice; I gladly handed my worries over. I surrendered. I felt I had no other choice other than to fall into faith. It was the only answer for me.

I do, however, remember the cab ride to the hospital, pulling up and seeing the doors for the first time. The private entrance to the cancer center was small and nondescript. How could such plain doors of glass change so many families' lives, I thought as I humbly walked through those doors of the Children's Hospital, knowing my life would never be the same again. I would no longer be the same person. I looked down at my shoes as I walked into the waiting room, feeling ridiculous wearing my new snakeskin high heels into this life-changing place. But they were the only shoes I had. I felt horrid: all dressed up to see my child, who had just been diagnosed with cancer. The first person I saw was my friend,

Dr. Jen. I've walked into that hospital hundreds of times since, into that crowded waiting room, but the first time, she was the first one I saw. On the lookout for me, she assured me that my daughter was in good hands, that her cancer was treatable. We would know in a matter of a few days exactly what kind of leukemia she had—once all of the tests came back.

"She will be okay," she assured me. If you're gonna have a kid with cancer, I definitely suggest having a friend who is a pediatric cancer doctor.

And so, it began, the three-year-long journey to heal my child. This new rollercoaster ride really changed me in ways I never thought possible. I grew into a different person almost overnight as my heart continued to break, leaving the old me behind.

My husband changed too. He couldn't hack being at the hospital. He was a blubbering mess, talking to everyone about nothing—it was weird and uncomfortable for our daughter. Children's hospitals are challenging places—people are scared, and the worry on the parents' faces is enough to crack anyone's heart right open, and that's exactly what it did. It cracked my heart open like a thin-shelled egg. I spilled over with empathy and compassion for the children and families. We often shared our children's stories of disease and the fears that came along with them. My husband, on the other hand, would show up at the hospital with a stack of Starbucks gift cards and randomly hand them out to nurses we didn't even know. He was trying, but at a loss of what to do. Imagine being with your five-year-old daughter, who's maybe twenty-five pounds at the time, barely able to move, vomiting and having diarrhea from the chemotherapy, and having random nurses come in to thank us for a twenty-dollar coffee card. Of course, they were just being nice, and they saw families like us every day. They were used to it, but we were not.

When one of the nurses would enter to say thanks, my face would be screaming back, "Get the fuck out of here!"

Words were not even needed. After that, both my daughter and I agreed we would go to the chemo treatments without Dave. He would stay home with Savvy, who was only two at the time, while I stayed for the overnight inpatient treatments. I was always on high alert after that, always ready at the drop of a hat to run my child to the hospital at even the smallest inclination of a fever.

My husband continued to be stoned.

This is where my dislike of him started to set in.

I had barely seen my bio dad since my wedding. Sam had just been discharged from the hospital, and he and his wife showed up in their newest fancy motorhome and parked in front of our beach house. I was exhausted trying to take care of house guests and my family while also trying to mentally wrap my head around the fact that my kid had just been diagnosed with leukemia.

My mother had just gone back to Utah after I screamed at her when she asked me how to get to Sea World. "Sea World? I'd yelled, "my daughter was just diagnosed with cancer less than three days ago, and you're asking me how to get to Sea World? Ask anyone else in the entire fucking city of San Diego, BUT DON'T ASK ME!" I'd gritted my teeth so hard, trying to keep from screaming at the top of my lungs or lurching for her jugular as I shut my daughter's hospital room door to walk my mom out. Her intentions were not ill willed; she only wanted to entertain Savvy, but needless to say, I was glad to see her go.

A week later, we brought Sam home from the hospital. Savvy's second birthday was just days away, but it would have to be postponed. Sam's immune system was compromised, which meant we could not have too many people around. Sam was small and frail and finally hungry from the steroids, and she wanted bacon. Lots, and lots of bacon.

"How can she eat so much bacon?" my bio dad would ask as I continued to cook the bacon. "Do you really think she should eat more bacon? Really, are you going to make her more bacon? Hey Kami, I really don't think you should be feeding her so much bacon!"

"GET THE FUCK OUT OF MY HOUSE!"

I don't remember if I actually said those words out loud. Probably not, with two small children present, but if not, I am quite certain my face said it loud and clear. Dave had deemed me Medusa, the snake lady, and maybe this time it was certainly true. Dad and his wife shortly packed up and left, never to come back. I hardly spoke to them after that. It was one thing for him to have picked on me, treating me like shit my whole life and always questioning why I would or would not do something, judging all my decisions about my life. He'd picked on me, and he could be so patronizing. Let's not forget the fact that he'd sexually abused me when I was barely eighteen! That had really fucked me up, and I thought I had let that go. But here, now, I was about to take his eyes out with just the look on my face for talking about my child's eating in that manner. My heart broke for my children and what was happening in both of their small frail lives, over which I had no control. I was sad, and scared.

Why were my parents so stupid, so uncaring, so unevolved? I was angry. Angry at anyone and everyone. My baby was sick, and I was scared and alone.

I had nobody.

Throughout Sam's treatment, she literally became the poster child for San Diego Children's Hospital. For years, they would be by our side, documenting and filming her progress. I wasn't quite sure how this happened, but when a woman showed up asking if they could film us, somehow I couldn't say no. She, too, was amazing, and on her own journey. She'd been born with severe rheumatoid arthritis that pretty much crippled her. I immediately connected with her. Her pain was not unlike mine. Her pain was on the outside for everyone to see. She inspired me and motivated me to persevere and hold my shit together. She was there for me in the midst of what one might call the tragedy of a lifetime, and I agreed to be filmed while in it. I shared my family's open wound for all to look at and take pity on. Somehow it was okay with us. They followed us around, filming and sharing our story to raise funds for the hospital. We were what I jokingly called the perfect-looking "High-Fiving White Family." Samantha, with her beautiful white-blonde hair and big blue eyes, was so young and innocent when diagnosed at age five—just a baby, really. This was every parent's worst nightmare—to have a child with cancer. I prayed more in those three years than I had in my entire life. Our community support was incredible. We were determined to get through this. Many children didn't. Some of our best little friends went to heaven. When Sam asked where they went, I let her know they'd gone home, but I failed to mention which home.

I meant heaven, but was that really my belief? My spiritual quest to find more answers continued, as did my gratitude for life and my own small family.

12

IT'S A LUV THING

Sam was finished with treatment—what a giant sigh of relief. She'd endured treatment like a champ, of course. This kid was so tough, she barely complained about anything. We had a big party at Nobu Sushi to celebrate. Dave gladly picked up the check for the twenty-five or so guests that came. We were all happy to leave the past behind us, and we welcomed the celebration of a new chapter. Sam did not want to talk about cancer or being sick ever again, so we tried hard not to. Cancer had been the center of all our lives for three long years, and we all needed some positive energy.

Savvy was starting kindergarten, and I was anxious for a creative outlet, a place where I could find healing and heal others in return. I was now living in such gratitude. My baby was alive, she was well, and she was healed. I was so thankful, so blissfully happy with my life and my two healthy, beautiful daughters, Savvy, now five, and Sam, eight.

After praying so hard for my child to live, I was a true believer in God and in my higher power. I had pulled out all the stops—life was glorious, and I wanted to live it that way. I would often ask questions of the universe and get the answers back through music, signs on the street, or people talking. I made it a point to be aware and curious about how the energy would show up, and sure enough, it always did. I knew to ask and to listen, to observe my surroundings and call in what I needed. I had given up my career five years earlier to stay home with my children, and I felt so blessed that I had made that decision.

Now, after Sam's treatment was over, I needed something creative to do again. I would often paint the walls of an entire room while my kids napped, but it was time to move onto other creative projects that would give me a little more in return than just a fresh color of paint.

We had some hefty leftover hospital bills, and I was tired of being in trouble for stupid shit around the house. I was tired of hearing about the laundry not being finished or the counters not being wiped off to perfection. Often there were still streaks that my husband would clean the second he walked into the house from work. The worst though, was the stainless-steel kitchen sink. Sometimes, I would laugh and think, "if I only got half as much attention as the kitchen sink, I might be happy." My husband wiped that thing spotless several times a day. I felt like my housework was micromanaged, and not in a good way. I knew how to make money and loved taking on creative projects. I was also ready for some fun and human connection, without the thick black cloud that hovered over my husband's head.

I wasn't sure what to do. I felt a need to express myself creatively, to utilize the energy flowing through me, but I wasn't sure how. So, I did what I always do when pondering a question—I sat in meditation waiting for the answers, pen and paper in hand, sitting on the overstuffed chair in my bathroom.

"Please, universe, tell me what I should be doing: what is my soul calling at this time? How can I serve others, connect, and show up in a fun, supportive, and positive way?" I sat and waited.

I had started working on manifesting. As I sat on the chair in my bathroom, I'd meditate and wait. This time I was asking the universe what I should do with my life.

"Rent a space" was what I wrote in my notebook.

I laughed to myself, writing down, "What is in this space?"

"Love, of course." The answer came so quickly, making me laugh again.

"Only items you LOVE," I wrote down.

What material things did I love anyway?

I wrote down "T-shirts, jeans, and jewelry—simple perfect items that people love and that would inspire healing by also sending a positive message." I would put my love and energy into these items, and those who wore them, and they would feel the special love I had put into my "luv things." I drove right to the space that I wanted, a sleepy little center that was once a motel. Now a couple of shops resided there. I envisioned the center thriving, and it wouldn't be long before that vision, too, would become my reality. My hairdresser, Nicole, had also said I should open a store, and I had thought she was crazy. Of course, our hairdressers often know us better than we know ourselves.

It was only a few months later that It's a luv thing boutique was born in Leucadia, California, a sleepy surf town on the Coast Highway 101. Chinese boxes were mailed out to twenty lovely ladies with tank tops that read, "the luv is coming," with an invitation inside to bring friends to the opening party. The big sign on the front of the store boldly read, "It's a luv thing, boutique de Leucadia."

On opening day, I sold $12K in volume. And I sold $550K the first year. Not too bad for opening a boutique on my credit cards with a lot of support and help from my husband and a few dear friends. I absolutely loved my work, but it took up a lot of time and energy, taking me away from my children. Manifesting was what I loved doing, and I practiced it daily. I woke up early, and while in the bathtub I would sit and bring awareness to my body. I would send the energy up my chakras, spinning the energy and making it bigger, enveloping myself in love. I would imagine this energy calling out to anyone who needed me, who needed love. I would envision miraculous things happening in the store with this giant energy of love. I opened myself up to experiences and people, and they would just come in at a time of need or celebration. They would just drop in to shop, and they would share beautiful stories of love, pain, inspiration, and heartbreak, often not knowing why they had stopped by in the first place. It was what I had wanted—to create a place where women could just be, relax, and feel heard and loved. A place for magic to happen, and it did. I had created my bliss. I had called it in.

This darling Luv thing boutique, which I opened only blocks from my house, was soon on fire. My kids were enrolled in elementary school just across the street and would come out and wave to me at recess and sometimes at lunch. I would often run across the tracks and find them on the playground or at the lunch tables, just to say hello, because—why not? I loved seeing their faces light up when they saw me. I could have taken a week or two off while both kids were healthy and back at school, to just chill and relax. But I had felt the need to get back to work and opened my store the first week Savvy started kindergarten.

Magical experiences started happening daily at my boutique. People would show up, not knowing why, and leave feeling connected and loved. The feeling was mutual. I felt as though what I was putting out was coming back tenfold. I put so much love and energy into everything in the store. I constantly blessed the products and those who would wear them. I designed T-shirts with spiritual sayings about love on them, and hand-cut hundreds and hundreds of velvet hearts for my "wear your heart on your sleeve" signature shirt.

I so loved my work. But the next thing I knew, I was in trouble with my husband for working—I really couldn't do anything right in his eyes. The kids and my husband would often drive up to the open double doors so the girls could say hello to me, and Nancy, who managed the store, once walked out to say hello to him and the girls. She walked back in, saying, "Wow, that was like walking into a brick wall, his energy was so thick, mean, and nasty."

"Yes, welcome to my world!" I said.

I couldn't do anything right according to Dave. He didn't like what I cooked, saying my meals were too healthy. He made fun of me constantly, picking at every little detail—the way I laughed and the outfits I wore. He even started making fun of me for being "spiritual" and encouraged the girls to follow suit. I had taken them to temple at the Self-Realization Fellowship center, the beautiful temple founded by Paramahansa Yogananda that was the core of the town we lived in. Dave and the kids never went back. But I went often, mostly to the weekly meditation. I immersed myself in deep meditation for the one- or two-hour session, during which I sat in silence with others who attended. It was so peaceful and full of pure beautiful energy that I longed to soak it in.

Dave, on the other hand, had a way of telling people what they wanted to hear. Around other people, he reflected back the perfect man. He would offer to do something for some kind soul, then after we left the situation, he would often comment about doing the exact opposite, saying something like "that guy was an asshole, I am not really going to help him." I knew his heart and actions didn't stand behind his words. This form of manipulation and lack of integrity shook me to my core. His inability to tell the truth made me feel as though I no longer knew the man. After Sam got better, I started pulling away, spending all my extra energy on my spiritual studies or my work. It was time to heal the traumas that ran so deep inside, instead of always trying to put a band-aid on things or run away and start a new life. That is what I had always done, but this time I was ready to do the work, ready to dive deep and heal the tough childhood traumas. I really needed to break the horrible chain before I, too, passed it on to my daughters.

13

I WANTED BIRTHDAY PRESENCE

SEPTEMBER 2007

Somehow, I'd always known that my husband and I would have a tragic ending, that he would turn his back on me or leave me in some way. I had openly discussed it with him. I really thought he would die young, leaving me to raise the children on my own. I wasn't quite sure how I knew, and I even asked him to renew our vows and take out additional life insurance, which he did. He even surprised me one year by making an appointment to be remarried at a darling little Baha'i Faith church in Molokai, Hawaii. I was so pleased with the thought he'd put into this; however, when we met the Baha'i people, they would not marry us. We were not qualified as we had not done the studies, nor did we know their beliefs, but we went to the service anyway, as they still wanted to celebrate us.

Dave sang me a lovely country song while playing the ukulele during the small church ceremony, as I quietly cried for our relationship—not tears of joy, like the others there might have thought. I knew our marriage would not last, and I still didn't know why—but I knew my faith would. I spent the next few days with the Baha'i family who ran the church, learning their stories and listening to their beliefs while my husband surfed. I loved how they shared their sacred stories of all faiths coming together in a circle, and how all the circles are all connected, as are all religions—only separated by man, not God. I also made a deep connection to the woman running the church. She was the kahuna, revered by the community. After spending several days with them, I left with an armload of interesting spiritual books, a heavy heart, and many blessings. It wasn't what I had come for, but I couldn't deny the gratitude I had for the new books, stories of faith, and connections with new friends.

My birthday was just around the corner. From the time I was ten, I'd always hated celebrating. I have no memory of having a fun birthday as a child. I hated playing all the stupid games. I usually had anxiety for weeks leading up to the day. I even have a picture to prove my early disdain for the dumb event. I was cute, all dressed up in my purple poncho with fringe trim and high ponytails, one a bit curlier than the other from sleeping with my pink spongy rollers. In the photo, you can see the perfectly straight part that ran down the back of my head, separating the ponytails—and my head bowed between my crisscross applesauce legs as I cried.

I always wondered why my mom had taken that picture. Why is it the only picture I had of my childhood birthday? Wasn't it *my* birthday? I'd wanted to do things my way that day—I cried, and that was that. I still didn't get my way, and I'd soon gotten used to it. I also got used to feeling alone, hence my early curiosity to seek something more, something bigger than myself—something or someone nurturing and loving. Instead of in people, I found it in nature, in meditation, and in my walks.

In September 2007, I had just redecorated our house and wanted to have a small dinner party for my birthday, with only two other couples. But my husband wanted the interiors painted professionally. It was as if he was negating my request with his condition. Sure, my painting wasn't perfect; the baby would often wake up in the middle of my paint project, so some areas were not so good, with a few drips here and there, overspray. You know—messy, yes, but still not horrible. He was often quite surprised to leave for work with a yellow kitchen and come home to an all-blue one. Then on to the next room I would go, needing something to do, something to create; that was always my answer.

"Okay then, let's get the house painted, and then can I have a dinner party?" I asked excitedly.

"Kami, there is absolutely no way you will find a painter to come in here and get this place finished before your birthday." That was all the challenge I needed. I headed to Home Depot to pick my paint colors, and within five minutes I met my painter—and a new best friend—Roberto.

Just days before my birthday, the house got perfectly painted.

My birthday came, and we had Trader Joe's frozen ravioli for dinner—no friends, no dinner party. There were no accolades for my hard work or the recent completion of the impossible painting job, no presents, and definitely no cake.

Nothing. He and the girls acknowledged that it was my birthday, yet they hadn't planned anything. I was hurt and tried to brush it off—I was already quite used to not being celebrated.

A week later, I was hosting one of my monthly shopping parties. I couldn't get the lights in the garden at the shop to work, so I went home to ask my husband if he could help. He was known for being "MacGyver," able to fix anything. I knew it would take him only minutes. The crazy landlords had insisted we also rent the small studio apartment and the backyard with our lease. Dave had built a beautiful deck, and we put in an amazing botanical garden, where I loved to hang out and throw huge monthly shopping parties to help pay for the extra rent the garden incurred. I was thrilled to have sunshine, plants, and flowers; things my custom home oddly lacked.

My husband was not happy with this request to help with the lights. He was quite furious. He had recently decided he was not going to help at the store anymore. He had started resenting it, resenting me. He was mad that I was always there and, I think, maybe a little jealous of the money I was making. Even though we shared all our finances, I had always been able to make more money than he had, and I think his ego was a bit bruised because of it.

I begged him to help. He finally walked over to the store to fix the garden lights, and he was even madder when he got back.

"Why didn't you tell me it was your birthday?" he asked.

I couldn't believe it. Like he didn't know my birthday had been last week? My girlfriend Sarah and I, birthdays only days apart, were going to have cake and champagne at the end of the shopping party, but that was all. Nancy must have told him we were celebrating my birthday.

"It isn't a big deal," I responded—of course, it hurt my feelings. Now he somehow felt obligated to come to the party.

He screamed at me, again pissed that I hadn't included him, which resulted in more crying from me. He'd forgotten my birthday, and now he was mad at me because of it? I tried to pull myself together while trying to brush off his verbal abuse. I put on some makeup and tried to be cute, and somehow, I mentally pulled myself together as I walked the two blocks to my store. Then, I got a little pissed off too, determined to show him what I was made of. I did my usual meditation on manifesting as I walked to the store, bringing my energy up and around me, envisioning myself in my store, people coming in, enjoying themselves, and being surrounded by the beauty and love I had worked so hard to project. Once there, I quite easily sold $10K in just a few hours. However, my husband was never very impressed by this. He had always grown up with money and had never felt a lack of it like I had. Dave arrived at the party all dressed up with a new 7 Diamonds shirt and a pretty little box in his hand. He was the ultimate show-off. In front of everyone, he said how wonderful and amazing I was, bragging about my awesomeness as he gave me an expensive ring he had just purchased from the jewelry store next door. If only he'd cared about ME as much as he cared about what those strangers thought of him, life would have been different between us, but this enormous difference between us had become an ugly monster that was now rearing its ugly head, and I was over it.

I was disgusted with this sudden display of attention that was meant for everyone but me. I took him into the office and said I was done. Just like that, I was finished. I could finally see through the shallow person I was married to. His way of manipulating any situation and coming out smelling like a rose was completely unsettling to me.

I still loved him, though I had been trying for months to connect, asking him to go to therapy, to talk, to have sex, any-thing! But it wasn't happening. He could not be present with me no matter how hard I tried. We rarely had sex. That had stopped over the past year. I always put a star on the calendar when we did. Trust me, I tried—even chasing him around naked didn't turn him on. Nothing like a naked turndown to really stop a girl's sexual confidence in its tracks. He was asleep when I got to bed and gone when I woke up. He would grunt at me if I touched him in his sleep. Even a little pat on the shoulder was dismissed, and kissing, of course, was completely off limits. The only connection we had in bed was usually just a low growl—and not the sexy kind—coming from my husband when I snored, followed by a push on my shoulder.

I was married but felt so alone. My husband was physically around, but he spent zero quality time with me. We were not connected, and I was over being treated like shit. I felt like my marriage was a facade—seemingly perfect on the outside but empty and fake on the inside. I wanted to be with people who were authentic—people who liked me just for being me, and liked my imperfect, whacky ways.

The night of the party at my shop, I decided to file for divorce.

Happy Birthday to me.

14

EBONY AND IVORY

One night, my friend Grace drove to L.A. to meet me for dinner and a slumber party. Her business was also on fire—the good old days, pre-recession. We decided to shop at a few boutiques in North Hollywood. Being a boutique owner myself, I loved checking out all the groovy little places in L.A., finding inspiration from the eclectic vibe that only a big city can offer. We walked into a small shop, and I found the most beautiful pair of hand carved wooden high heels ever. Dainty, little Swarovski crystals made up the buckle across the toes.

"Such a bargain," I said sarcastically, "on sale for only five-hundy." I didn't care, I had to have them. So absurd, I think now, looking back.

"Ha, I'll probably find a new man in my life, wearing these shoes, and I would like a tall, beautiful black man who is spiritually conscious and has a lot of money." I laughed as I said it. My girlfriend Grace looked at me funny, with one eyebrow raised questioning me. She knew I was not a material girl.

"It might take a lot of money to do the kind of world healing I dream of doing," I said.

I bought the shoes. We had dinner at a sushi place just across the street from the Mondrian, a swanky, upscale hotel with modern décor and a pool surrounded by a glass wall that overlooked the city. I loved the place, and I loved the new shoes I had just bought. Fun and good times were on the agenda. We met a big group of hot men in their forties sitting at the table next to ours. They were all sweet and quite good-looking, but nobody was of any interest. They told us about a few cool clubs close by and invited us to join them, so I thought, why not? Grace was recently divorced herself, and now that I had filed for divorce, we were curious to see what was "out there" in the world of single men.

We went to the first club they'd mentioned, and I saw him the second I walked in. I actually walked right up to him confidently and said, "You sure are a beautiful man, why are you wearing such an ugly shirt?"

He was a tall, good-looking black man, of course. He had thick, perfect dreadlocks that swept just above his shoulders. He was wearing dark jeans, fancy shoes, and an old, beat-up royal blue Puma T-shirt. I didn't think they went together well.

"But did you see my shoes?" he asked.

"Oh yeah, I saw your Italian leather shoes," I said, not missing a beat. "And did you see *my* new shoes?" I asked, looking down. My jeans were long flares, of course, and they kind of hid my new, sparkly shoes.

"Ah, what gorgeous shoes! Roll up your jeans and dance in those pretty shoes."

I giggled as he kneeled down and helped me roll up the bottom of my jeans. This simple Cinderella gesture really moved me. We continued to dance without talking for the next half hour or more, having so much fun, laughing and smiling. His energy pretty much bowled me right over, and his piercing eyes held something intense and familiar. The music finally stopped, and I asked him his name.

"Ebony," he said.

"Ebony?" I laughed out loud, looking down at my white top, white skin, and long, straight white-blonde hair. "Then who the fuck am I? Ivory?"

Chills went up my entire body. It wasn't a sexual connection—it was more of a spiritual connection, but it was real and extremely powerful.

Light and dark, ebony and ivory, up and down, forwards and backwards. Good and evil—duality—you cannot have one without the other.

He was a gorgeous, confident man with a vibe that knocked the wind out of me. The perfect universal pull, I thought.

It pulled me, all right. It was the kind of connection I had believed in, one I had anticipated, wanted, and longed for. Our energies together were somehow synergistic and pure. We closed down the bar, and he gave me a ride back to the hotel in his fancy black Mercedes and asked for my number. This time I freely gave it out.

A few days later, our spiritual banter was still going strong. I could finally speak what felt like my truth with him without being judged or shamed for my difference of opinion. I shared how I felt that we were all so sadly asleep to what was really going on in the world, too busy to look up or to look outside of the bubble we had created for ourselves. We rarely looked outside of the box for what was important in life, only to look up one day and wonder what it was all for? What was life all about? What did I learn, how did I grow, how did I serve? Was I my best self? These were the deep conversations Ebony and I were having. Conversations about respect for ourselves and for those around us.

I loved how easy it was to talk about life, love, and fear and the energetic frequencies they all held. I believed that the government, and the people they worked for, knew about these energies and wanted to keep the rest of the world from knowing about them. They wanted to keep us enslaved in our own fears—afraid to question much and afraid of our own unlimited potential to heal and have abundance.

I longed to converse about deeper things besides the everyday physical aspects of what my family needed or what I was making for dinner. I wanted more; I craved substance and understanding. I longed for true, unconditional love and a spiritual connection.

I was still living at home when I started talking with Ebony on the phone. A few days later, I went for a walk and talked on the phone with him—I justified that it was fairly safe to just have a phone conversation with him; besides, he was out of town traveling for his work. I talked of wanting to go to the sacred sites of the planet—places like Lake Titicaca, in Peru; Stonehenge; and Egypt. In years past, anytime a customer or friend traveled, I would send them with one of the many crystals that adorned my store, asking them to plant it somewhere special, giving back love, gratitude, and healing to Mother Earth. My intentions were of helping restore the crystal grid of the planet. Nicole, my hairdresser, the one who talked me into opening my It's a luv thing store in the first place, even took a crystal to Tulum, Mexico, one of my favorite places, hiding it between some rocks in a sacred sweat lodge. There, every day at 11:11, prayers were offered up to the divine from the shaman who held space in the sweat lodge. Of course, I was thrilled about this, being forever in search of the number 1111 and the meaning these numbers held. I told Ebony how thrilled this prayer made me, and the story of all the magical crystals being sent out and activated with love by the people planting them with intention. I was always so happy to hear the journey and story of each crystal, and I somehow knew they were helping to activate the Earth's Crystalline Grid. This grid would eventually help the entire planet ascend to a new 5D earth. I longed to travel to the major portals of this grid, which were also known as the seven chakras of the planet, to plant my own love and healing there.

Ebony didn't make fun of me when I shared stories of my spiritual practices or what I was learning after endless hours of research down the rabbit hole of truth. We shared opinions about what was going on in the corporate world—how the rich elite were mindfully monopolizing every aspect of the world we lived in, while we went about our simple, small-thinking lives feeling like we had a say, a "vote." We talked about the music industry, Hollywood, and the mainstream media, all so full of control and weirdness. No wonder nobody really wanted to know what was going on. We were so full of distractions and so affected by censorship, from which we all gladly took the bait—hook, line, and sinker. Humanity was such an easy fish to fry. We enjoyed our ignorant bliss and would do just about anything to defend it. Nope, nobody really wanted to hear about the money, power, and control that kept the population steeped in fear and division. This form of mental slavery definitely kept us from stepping into our highest and best selves. Most of the population did not even realize the infinite possibilities that we were capable of. But the people running the world sure knew and would do just about anything to keep the secret.

I had longed for this kind of banter, to have someone with whom to discuss these sorts of topics. With Ebony, I was finally getting it. Maybe I was ahead of trend. Back then, nobody thought these conversations were as interesting as I did. It was 2007, after all. When would people get it? When would everyone realize the constant control that surrounded us from the government, the corporations, and big pharma—what and how to believe all spoon fed to us through media, which influenced the way we lived, the way we thought, and even the foods we ate and drank, which were mostly poison? Very few seemed to care or hear about my so-called conspiracies. But Ebony did.

Unfortunately, this new connection didn't last long. All this intense energy was too much for me to absorb. Within just a few days of meeting him, I went to the mental hospital for the first time. Soon every friend of mine was calling him to ask if he had drugged me or if he did something or said something to send me there. Who could blame the poor guy—we had barely met, and then off to the loony bin I went. I wasn't crazy, but, to me, the world sure as hell was. I just looked at things differently, saw the world in a different light, and wanted to tell everyone about it. The opening and comfort I felt when talking to Ebony had shaken me. It had opened me up to a different way of seeing the world—a world of unconditional love and the possibility to live in a higher dimension of love and manifestation. I was overwhelmed and thrilled to feel this way with such freedom and bliss, and soon off the planet I flew.

Looking back, I wonder if he was a dark angel who swept in to push me off my path.

PART THREE

15

ER PARTY

After hours of hanging out at the Meditation Gardens, more friends showed up, and then the police, and then another two friends, both of whom were doctors. One practiced Western medicine and one was a psychologist who practiced Eastern spiritual philosophies. I explained to both of them that it was time to merge the philosophies of Eastern and Western medicines in order to actually get to the core of real healing! All this while I was singing, "Ebony and Ivory, together in perfect harmony . . ." They weren't buying it.

My friends talked me into getting in a car and said that one of them would give me a ride. But we didn't go to a hotel like I wanted. I knew that I needed to get grounded and make sense out of all of this intense energy running through my body. Instead, we went to the emergency room. Oh, this was an emergency all right. But this was not that kind of emergency, I thought, more of an emergence.

I had been obsessed with numerology for years, so I already knew that everything was about the numbers. The entire universe was comprised of a mathematical equation, unfolding and continuing in mathematical perfection. The whole world had been laid out on an amazing mathematical grid. All sacred sights and wonders of the world, including Washington D.C., fell onto this perfect mathematical grid known as the Ley Lines. These energetic Ley Lines were all connected, as was everything in the universe. I found it fascinating that everything was lined up so perfectly. Engineering at the time these sacred sites were built was still beyond anything we are capable of today.

Not only was everything connected, but it was also a reflection. Maybe this was the 1111 that I had been looking for all those years, the Parallel Universe, the As Above so Below, all of which we had heard about so often from the Good Book we know as the Bible.

Everything we put out in the world, which is above, rains down on us in our physical manifestation—the below.

The opposite of 911 would be 119. These numbers had started showing up again and again everywhere I went. Was I emerging? Was I enlightened? I had spent the past twenty or more years studying and reading about almost every practice of spirituality I could get my hands on. Was it any surprise really, with all this studying, that it could actually have been coming true—that we could actually create Heaven on Earth, or even our own Hell, whichever way we decided to look at it—or cocreate the world we all currently coexisted in? Wasn't it all just a matter of one's perspective? That whatever we believed we really did receive? These were all the things that I was in deep contemplation about as we arrived at the emergency room.

My heaven came to a quick halt as all my friends piled into the tiny emergency room. "So, this is the party you ladies want to be having with me?" I said. "A hotel really would have been much better."

After what felt like eons at the ER, all tests came back negative. There was nothing in my system but small traces of THC. No alcohol, no drugs—nothing. My room was filled with worried lady friends who had now sent out for food because we had been there so long. But I wasn't interested in food. My celestial friend looked like hell as she rubbed the hair under her beanie and looked around at all my lady friends, hoping someone had an answer to my "ailments." Ali, my voice-of-reason friend, had just showed up looking cold, and she had a worried look on her face, but she still hadn't said much since she arrived. I could tell she was trying to figure out how to solve this problem, but she couldn't—it was too late. The damage had been done, and the paperwork had been filed. I took off my cashmere socks and gave them to her. Her face lit up, and Celestial cried even more.

"You're fine," Ali said. "You even knew I was cold."

"Yes," I said, "and these are the socks Celestial gave me for Christmas, so make sure I get them back."

Phones were dying, and my concern and fear of the phones confirmed my craziness, as I talked of them listening to us, soon to be tracking us like animals. Hadn't "they" already been poisoning us with the nasty processed food and TV programs? "They" didn't even hide the fact they were programming us; they just openly called them "programs." Like the Ley Lines and sacred sites, they were not hidden but in plain sight. Our vocabulary reflected this: spell—ing our words, openly casting spells—everything before us was right in plain sight, and everything in the universe suddenly made more sense. Except for the fact that I always felt so alone in my thinking, especially back then in 2007.

I looked up at poor Celestial. I had thought she would have understood me better, but then again, she had just watched me masturbate, sing, walk a brick fence, and run into the middle of the street. I'd also talked her into meditating with me on the hill. I'd told her that once we got to a higher state of consciousness, we wouldn't notice the hill at all; that we could become one with the hill and with the plants and the energies that surrounded us in unconditional love. Better yet, we could become one with our higher selves in that magic sweet spot that could enable us to manifest on a moment's notice. Sexual energy had something to do with this: letting go to the point of elevating oneself to a high enough state of consciousness that you became more in unison with the planet, with creation.

I wasn't quite sure as I was still absorbing all this information pouring into me as well. But I would have plenty of time to meditate, to drop in, to find the answers that had put me here in the first place, so I surrendered.

I gave my girlfriends a parade wave as the paramedics strapped me onto a gurney and wheeled me into the ambulance that would drive me from the medical hospital to the mental hospital in downtown San Diego. This sure was a far fucking cry from the Ritz Carlton, which I easily could have paid for instead of this current ride. Imagine the champagne my girlfriends and I could have drunk in three days for $7,000, which was the price of the ambulance ride plus my three-day stay at the mental hospital. I never saw or spoke to Celestial again.

16

OFF TO THE LOONY BIN

I fell back into my deep meditation as they drove me downtown to the behavioral clinic. I was still pretty "high on life," even after the eventful day of police, doctors, concerned friends, and what I thought was actual craziness. I calmly tried to explain myself to the admitting nurse. "Right now, both sides of my brain are firing at the same time," I shared, "this enables me to download information from the Akashic records."

The Akashic records are kind of like the iCloud of everyone's soul path, past, present, and future. I had been eating super clean, not drinking any alcohol, and meditating, studying, and experimenting with all kinds of spiritual belief systems and energetic frequencies. I had been participating in sound healings, chanting, and listening to music played at certain frequencies. I lit candles, saged, worked with crystals, and had a fairly impressive altar, which I tended to daily. I loved learning about the intricacies of the planet and the universe and how everything was a reflection yet also magnetic.

It's simple, actually, and so are we.

This "tapping in" is quite normal for Buddhist monks during meditation as well as practitioners of many other indigenous spiritual belief systems. But here in the United States? Well, that's just plain craziness. Go ahead and just sign here to be admitted to the mental hospital if you don't go along with the norms of society!

Why is it so normal for our computers to tap into the iCloud, but to use your brain to get information is considered crazy?

You could almost hear the rolling of the nurse's eyes as she thought, yep, we have another crazy one here. I had been frying phones, computers, printers, and many light switches for quite some time now. The lights at home and in the boutique would flicker many times when I went to switch them on or off. The computer printer would die when I tried to use it, and phones all around me were suddenly dying. At least I knew the energy going through me was real. I filled out the paperwork and looked forward to the tests they would soon run to confirm my brilliance.

Wrong. I was really, really wrong.

Being admitted felt like I was going to jail. It was late at night, and I was sent to a room with a roommate. It was scary, smelly, dark, and dank with garbage all over. My roommate was an old woman who was snoring and talking in her sleep in some kind of foreign language. I was certainly not up for this, but I was determined to rise above it. I settled in on the hard mattress, back straight against the cold concrete wall as I climbed deeper inside myself, meditating and crying out telepathically. I was actually crying and screaming out to the ethereal field, sending telepathic messages to anyone who would pick up. "Please, please, come and rescue me."

One friend, Sarah, did come to visit the next morning, but I was still deep in my meditation and didn't want to be bothered by her. "You don't need to worry about me," I had told her. "I am busy talking to Quan Yin and Buddha, and I can't visit with you right now," I said.

Oh, it must have been interesting from her perspective, observing this odd behavior from her once fun and funny friend. She was worried, I could tell, as she sat there quietly and listened. Her signature red lipstick was perfect, as always, although the way her lips curved oddly to one side, I knew that she was concerned. But she didn't really know what to say or do as I dismissed her.

That afternoon, the floor nurse came in with medication that I wouldn't take, and I noticed her name tag said "Kami."

"Kami, huh? Is this some kind of joke?" I said.

"Why would it be a joke?" she asked.

"Well, I am learning that everything is a mere reflection of ourselves, mirroring back to us what we are putting out, and I do find it odd that your name is Kami."

"Really? Well, do you know what our name means?" she asked.

"No." I shook my head.

"It means God in Japanese," she said. "The Kami is a very revered, hidden God energy in the Japanese tradition."

I had done a lot of studying, but this was news to me. Japanese spiritually was something that I hadn't delved into.

I started laughing out loud. She wanted to know what was so funny.

"So, here I am, channeling all these incredible guides, sages, shamans, and archetypes, downloading God-like information. And you're telling me my name means God?"

It was just too much, even for me. I mean, you just can't make this shit up. I was in the mental hospital downloading information on how to step into our God-selves.

This means that everything we see, believe, and think is just our projection and our reflection—a creative manifestation portraying ourselves as God as us. We are the ultimate creators in this life, whoever we are showing up as in this lifetime, in the here and now. God is everyone and everything, and everything is just a reflection of what we are energetically putting out.

And my nurse's name was also Kami? She was certainly my reflection in my here and now.

I often said I was a student of everything and a master of nothing. I just loved learning about these sorts of things. I was also into quantum physics, Buddhism, Hinduism, and Kabbalah. I found shamanic studies fascinating and had traveled into a few jungles for shamanic healings and even psychic surgery—where the shaman removed impurities and disease without cutting a person open. I had traveled and attended Kabbalah services—I had even stood next to Demi Moore and Ashton Kutcher once while at Shabbat on the East Coast. I proudly owned the entire volume of the Zohar, the sacred text in Hebrew of the tree of life.

The mental hospital wasn't the first time or place where I had really contemplated who I was and the energy surrounding my name. Earlier in the year, while attending a Bat Mitzvah for a darling girl in our neighborhood, the rabbi had wanted to talk to me afterward. He had asked who I was. I had caught his attention energetically too many times while he was speaking. Looking down before we caught eyes, he even said out loud, "What's going on over here? I keep getting distracted," pointing in my direction while he spoke. After the service he left the people he was chatting with to come and meet me.

"Who are you?" he asked right away. "I just left a group of people in the middle of a conversation to come over and meet you. Your presence is so strong, and your energy kept disrupting me during temple," he continued. I didn't really have an answer for him.

My energy was big. Too big. I had been working on my energetic field—trying to raise my vibration in order to help heal my child, but I didn't know how to contain it or really work with it. I shrugged my shoulders and said, "i am kami?" I told him I was doing a lot of studying, praying, and meditating. What else could I say? He gave me his card to come and see him and then went back to his friends.

Shortly thereafter, another man came over to talk with me. He wanted to know where I went to temple.

"I don't go to temple. I'm not Jewish," I said.

"Then how do you know all of those sacred texts? I watched you chanting all the prayers. They are all in Hebrew."

Honestly, I didn't know the answer any better than he did. I had just opened my heart, my energy, my mouth, and the words just came out. Yes, in Hebrew. I couldn't explain it. I mean, yes, I had been scanning the Zohar in Hebrew for years, but I didn't think that was it. I attributed it to the collective of the group that was attending. By my being in tune, I had jumped into their focused energy source. I obviously did not speak Hebrew, but I had sure loved how it felt when I sang it. It was old, familiar, and somehow part of me.

With the nurse, I couldn't quit laughing at the fact that my name also meant God, the hidden energy in everything. So, I pondered, were we all aspects of God? Was this what I was trying to wrap my head around?

The answer came quickly: "Yes!"

"Or maybe this is just what it means to be fucking crazy," said my self-doubt. After all, I was in the mental hospital.

17

UNCOUPLING

No matter how positive you think you are going to be, and no matter how much time you spend "consciously uncoupling," if you have kids, it's going to suck. I so wish we had at least continued living together in our family house to raise the children as a family unit. I wish I could have, but that trend hadn't really started yet, and for once, I wasn't ahead of trend. Besides, I really wanted distance between my husband and me. He had threatened to take the girls away if I left him. I didn't think he would really do it, so I rented a fancy apartment with a panoramic ocean view and planned to fill it with brand-new furniture that I couldn't wait to shop for. I barely took anything from the house, except for my clothes and my antique vanity. Little did I know we were on the verge of hitting a hideous recession.

Or did I know? The previous year I had told Dave that we should sell our house, downsize, and move to Hawaii. I had offered it up because I thought that was what my husband wanted—it was all he talked about, retiring and moving to Hawaii. If he was happy, I could be happy, I reasoned. But he had said no. Earlier that year, I'd had a very strong urge to sell our house. The house down the street had just sold for close to two million, and our house was ten years newer. Having paid for most of the construction with the fat paychecks I had been making over the years in the surf industry, our mortgage was quite small. With the cool one mil in profit, we could have moved our family to Molokai, Hawaii, where my husband dreamed of building a small house and retiring. We could have a simple, beautiful life; he wouldn't have to work. I could fly back once a month and keep my thriving clothing boutique business going.

We were about to be in escrow on a house in Palm Springs, and we had property in Hawaii, a big house at the beach, and two beautiful, healthy daughters. Most importantly, we had one daughter who was currently in remission after a three-year battle with leukemia. Having her be healthy was a huge fucking deal. All should've been good in the world—our hearts should've been bursting open, full of gratitude and bliss. If we could get through having a child with cancer, we should've been able to get through anything. We should have had a whole new perspective on the world, one full of gratitude, beauty, and grace. I thought selling our house was a fantastic idea, and I couldn't wait to share this new grand plan with my husband.

Dave had been unhappy for what seemed like years now. He was always tired, complaining constantly, and I couldn't stand it. I wanted to fix his problems—fix him. I wanted to stop the incessant complaining and darkness that came into a room well before he even entered it himself. "I just have too much going on" was his consistent response. Yet, he had too much going on all the time.

As much as I tried to overcompensate for his negativity by being positive, I felt overwhelmed by his gloomy moods, and it was often hard to shift the energy in the house. I was tired of the black cloud that constantly hovered, threatening to burst into a dark torrential downpour at any given moment. I was also tired of the way he constantly belittled me and the passive aggressive comments he would often make in front of the girls. I was tired of it, and quite thrilled with my newest solution to fix things.

So, I climbed into the hot tub with him to tell him of my brilliant idea. I hated hot tubs—I was allergic to chlorine. But I wanted his attention, so I brought him coffee and climbed in to tell him of my recent grand plan to alleviate his stress and give him what he had dreamed of.

"No way!" he said rather harshly. "Why would we want to sell the Rock?" (He fondly called our house "the Rock"). It wasn't going to happen; I wasn't going to win on this one. It was a hard no. We rarely agreed on much those days. I basically had to chase him around the house hoping for a conversation, connection, a single ounce of attention and affection, even sex. Nope, he didn't even want sex. I was crushed. I knew I had settled, marrying a man who didn't like kissing. Sometimes I felt like I repulsed him. He often pulled away when I touched him, shuddering as if bothered by my affection or even my presence. I was glad to be done.

Dave had tried to smooth things over once after I returned from the looney bin. We had gone out to dinner with the kids at one of our favorite Mexican restaurants, pretending everything was normal. He'd tried to hold my hand, but it wasn't a kind or compassionate handholding. It was more like "I will control you, let's move on." Basically, it was more of a demand than a plea. I pushed his hand away, and the girls saw my actions, and I saw the scared look of concern on their faces. We all shared in the pain, and this wasn't going to be good or easy for anyone. I had tried to get through the holidays, sleeping in the playroom, but I was packed up and ready to leave the day after Christmas. I would have stayed—even sleeping in the playroom indefinitely would have been the better option—had I known what he'd do. But I wanted my own space, free of the crunching eggshells I currently walked on.

How many times over the years had I talked friends out of divorce, often offering advice for that exact reason, that it was so hard on the kids? But you can't always see your own shit when you are in it and need another perspective. Over the years I had chatted with friends and many customers about divorce. But I didn't ask for any advice. I had made a rash decision, and it was done. I painted the front door of my new rental red and shopped my ass off at Z Gallery, the high-end furniture store which was my current fave. I was so excited to feel freedom in my own space, and the peace of being away from Dave. My kids were not so excited, though. They were broken by the news of divorce, which was bad enough, but it was even worse being followed by the news that their mother had a mental illness.

While I was in the loon, my husband and my friend the Eastern philosophy doctor had sat my children down to tell them their mother was mentally ill, that I had just been diagnosed with bipolar disorder. Then, Dave had packed up the children, my computer, and all our financial information and gone to Laguna Beach, a few towns away, to his sisters. Worried what else I might be up to, as I had always handled the family's finances, Dave was checking everything. I arrived home from the mental hospital to a lonely house, and on my cleared-out desk sat $200 in cash left there from my husband. Had I just passed Go? Had my life just become a mean game? The money looked so odd, intentionally all fanned out on my desk like Monopoly money.

Now, neither Sam nor Savvy, ten and eight, wanted to come to my new house, as fun as I tried to make it. Sam, my strong-willed oldest, would hardly visit, and my husband refused to adhere to the custody arrangements, telling the girls they could come and go as they pleased, giving the children the choice and all the control.

I felt defeated.

Samantha, in particular, was not happy with me. Our personalities started clashing—her big, bold personality with a mean, sassy edge easily ran over my small, destroyed one that had arrived home last year from the mental hospital.

As we went through the divorce, my husband also let the girls know that if they didn't want to be around me or live with me, they didn't have to. Now they feared me, pushed me away, and treated me differently. How could our bond have been broken so easily?

Repeating the whole "who's your daddy" line that Dave had said to both of them since they were toddlers was just one of the many ways in which he had programmed our children. He also gave them blue Gatorade and other junk food that I did not approve of and then let them watch endless hours of television. I hadn't realized he had been alienating them from me since they were babies. I felt like a victim, and I wore it well as I started my slow sprialing descent towards depression.

Would it not have been better for the children, when I was in the hospital and they were only seven and nine, to tell them I'd had a bad fever—that I was contagious and would be home in a few days? Where was "the way of compassion" from Dave while dealing with our children? Or with me?

Dave hadn't even visited me in the mental hospital back then—how did he know how I was behaving? And he had recently threatened to take my children away if I left him. Maybe, just maybe, that's what had sent me to the loon in the first place.

Had I manifested that, too, or had his threats to take away my children gotten under my skin? Where was the strong, powerful, beautiful woman I once was? I was still here, dying from the inside out. First I had an unhappy marriage and now children who were wary of me. Withering with each missed visit from my kids, my once big, full heart silently broke into a million tiny little pieces.

This new sadness about my girls pushed me to work on myself even more. I saw more healers, energy workers, shamans, and tarot readers. I Reiki-trained and mastered. I went on yoga retreats, spiritual retreats, and trainings. just so I could learn about the healing energies. I chanted, I prayed, and I meditated. I sat in women's circles, I sat in Ayahuasca ceremonies, I did charity work, and I volunteered and made friends with all the local homeless people. I would do about anything to fill myself up, but nothing worked. I was so uncomfortable in my own skin; I had a hard time being present with the girls, and they felt it.

All I longed for was to reconnect with my daughters.

If this wasn't challenging enough, the recession hit full force right after I moved out in January. This sudden shift of business might as well have been a tidal wave to my already faltering business. Depleted of self-confidence from not seeing my children, both my business and I really started to slide. After only a couple of years, I moved out of my swanky apartment and into the studio apartment behind my store. This move embarrassed my children. My bohemian lifestyle started way before Bohème was cool, and at the time, it wasn't a good thing.

The move into the studio helped me recuperate financially for a while; then I decided to move my store, downsizing to reflect the ever-changing economy. This lasted a couple more years before I downsized again to a mobile boutique. (Again, way ahead of trend). I bought a 1971 red Volkswagen bus and decked it out with hot pink fur, gold shelving, and gold-embossed, cream vinyl wall coverings. People certainly didn't understand my bus or the pop-up concept—It's a luv thing was the first mobile boutique in California. There were only four other mobile boutiques in the country when I started. But my excitement to talk about shallow things such as dresses, fashion, and VW busses had fled with the economy. I couldn't care less, and it showed. I should have, though, as my savings were almost gone. I soon began to panic about my finances.

Downsizing to a mobile boutique was okay, but that meant I was the only one having to show up with my game on. Ordinarily, I would have thrown myself into work, trying to bury my grief, but it was too big and I couldn't shake it. I wished I still had employees to work for me and make money while I stayed at home with my broken heart. Being ahead of a trend isn't always fun, nor for the faint of heart, and this time I wasn't strong enough. I felt like a peddler, and I hated it.

Before the divorce, I had pulled a pretty big chunk of change from my IRA to invest into a retirement property in Palm Springs. My financial planner had been my accountant, and I was used to her handling everything. The funds that I let fall out of escrow were not mentioned when I filed my taxes—not on purpose, but my head was hardly on my taxes. I had little control over any part of my life at the time. However, my failure to disclose caused a red flag and an audit with the IRS, and with all the moving and craziness in my life, I no longer had all the paperwork to substantiate my expenses and income.

This would soon become one of my worst financial downfalls.

18

OFF TO THE LOON, TAKE TWO

I couldn't work on myself fast enough or hard enough over the next few years. Weekly acupuncture certainly saved my life. Lucky they still took me after the time I went into one of the treatment rooms during a "state" to set up a room for Jesus. Once again, I was channeling all kinds of sages and great archetypes. I was supposed to be meeting my shaman and some other friends soon in Peru for an Ayahuasca ceremony, but the sudden drop off in my finances stopped me in my tracks. I couldn't pay my 40K Amex bill. In one day of being late, I lost the 350,0000 points I had been saving for travel. So, of course, that put the final kibosh on going to Peru. However, as soon as the Ayahuasca ceremony started there, my soul dropped into a deep, almost walking, meditation. I felt as if I was physically there. I was journeying all right, but I was not in a safe or sacred contained space where channeling was welcomed, even revered. I wasn't even on Ayahuasca. I was home in my small beach town, and I hadn't planned to fly off the planet again.

I had planned, however, to sit in another circle locally with some spiritual sisters and another teacher. This was a very auspicious time, as 2012 was just around the corner, and many spiritual seekers anticipated the energetic shift that would come along with the year. Many circles were gathering all over the world in sacred meditation and ceremony. I had recently spent the last of my extra cash in Tulum, Mexico, in March, on a ten-day, intense spiritual retreat with this teacher, during which many coincidences occurred.

While in Tulum, everything had been all about the snake—the serpent—the shedding of one's skin to grow and evolve. In my dreams and on my walks, I saw snakes and a giant statue of a snake god. Wasn't it the snake (Satan) that tempted Adam and Eve into eating from the tree of knowledge? Wasn't it this divine action that opened them up to understanding language and higher means of learning? Did other people contemplate such things like this as I did?

My roommate on the Tulum retreat had just finished reading *Serpent of Light: Beyond 2012*, so she passed it on to me. We finished up the retreat and were flying home while I was still reading the book. Our flight was on March 21, the spring equinox, at sunset. At the exact same time, I was reading a chapter in this book about the serpent of light, in which the snake shows his shadow when the sun hits the revered Chichen Itza temple at sunset on the equinox. Right then, the airplane captain says over the loudspeaker, "Ladies and gentlemen, we are now flying over the Chichen Itza temple; today is the day people come from all over the world to see this amazing shadow displayed from the heavens."

Thin, the veil was getting very, very thin, I thought to myself. I felt the universe was screaming at me on all levels to take this shadow-self a little more seriously. The shadow-self represented the dark side of life, our trauma. This continuous showing up of the snake felt like a warning. Its dark shadow would soon be cast on my small, yet vulnerable life.

A week later, Savvy was working on a big poster for the talent show at school. I ended up staying up all night to work on it, or so I thought. I was totally not myself at all—I hadn't slept much that night. The painting, the lack of sleep, and the looming fear of what I would do with my life pushed me further into the ethereal world and out of my body. After getting the kids off to school, I came back home to straighten up the house. Only I didn't do that. I energetically cleaned it—taking every single tiny object that I picked up and connecting it to another, creating an almost mandala-like art piece with the items I pulled out of my drawers. I somehow needed to know in my own mind that everything was connected, no matter what the circumstance.

Maria, my spiritual teacher from Mexico, who had just flown into town, heard I was "out there" and had stopped to visit me at my apartment. After the brief tour of my giant mandala-art made of crap, she asked one of my spiritual sisters, Heidi, to bring me to where Maria would be staying. Upon arriving, I was awestruck to see the circle that was set up showing the portraits of the lineage of many great sages from the past. I felt as though something was getting passed on to me, and I was thrilled with anticipation. Maria did energy work on me for what felt like forever, and then she put her hand over my solar plexus, the third chakra, where a person's power is held. As soon as she touched me, I started screaming.

"Give me my egg, Give me my egg!" As I screamed, I envisioned Stacey, a beautiful, spiritual male friend of mine with whom I'd recently had a very strange connection while at his house. I had still been in an "out of body state." The state was like being in a very deep meditation—aware, but not really in control. It was kind of like watching a movie but watching yourself as an actor in the movie.

While at Stacey's house a few weeks before, I had been looking for a picture of Jesus, and I'd gone all over his house looking. Once I found it, I relaxed. When we had first met, we dated for a while, but we were now just friends, and he was keeping an eye on me as I had told him I was not quite okay. He lived in downtown San Diego, so I was spending the night.

He was next to me in his bed, and we were both fully clothed. I felt this powerful kundalini energy exchange between the two of us. It was as if I could see the rainbow energy of his soul arcing from his stomach and going into mine. I woke up the next morning feeling grounded and fine. I hadn't thought much about the incident until Maria's energy work, when I was suddenly screaming for my egg, and I didn't know why.

I finally calmed down from the energy work as my teacher took her hands from my stomach and left the room. I got up from the massage table feeling so much better, but not completely in my body just yet. I walked into the living room to put on my shoes. My teacher came out, said nothing, and handed me a rock. Not just any rock. It was a black, smooth, shiny, oval one, with many tiny white flecks. There it was, a beautiful, perfectly shaped black egg. She turned around with a not-so-happy demeanor and went back to her guest room, dismissing Heidi and me without a word. Was this the item I had wanted—a sacred object that was being passed down to me? But what did it mean? I wasn't really sure, but I was very happy with the gift. I was tired, and I was ready to go home.

I got in the car, thinking that my friend Heidi, who I had just been in Mexico with on the ten-day spiritual retreat, was doing just that: taking me home. But apparently, she had called my ex while I was being worked on by Maria, and they had all decided I should go back to the mental hospital.

As we drove into the emergency entrance of the hospital, I asked Heidi, "What are we doing here?" She told me that her husband worked there and that we needed to stop in and check on him. I shook my head, so very confused at the vague answers, but I didn't really care. I had my egg.

I was wondering if snakes ate eggs when I looked up and said, 'Wait, What? Why would your husband be here, at the hospital?"

She said again that he worked there. I shook my head again.

"No, your husband works in the surf industry," I answered back. I mean, I was high-as-fuck in the ethers, but I wasn't stupid. Having worked in the surf industry for many years, myself, I knew her husband. I trusted her—she herself was on track to soon become a spiritual teacher. I was so confused, but still trusted her.

Then Linda, another friend, showed up at the emergency room. I begged them both to take me home. I needed to be at my daughter's talent show in the morning. I couldn't miss it. Linda assured me my kids would be fine, and the nurse gave me a hospital gown to put on, and Linda packed up my clothes from the chair next to me at the ER. She left me with a pink rose quartz crystal, explaining to the nurse that the crystal would make me feel better. What would have made me feel better would have been if she'd taken me home, and I was not sure why she took my clothes. I was so confused, unable to get myself grounded.

So, once again, I was in the ambulance driving downtown to the mental hospital. This was what my spiritual friends and ex-husband felt was best for me? Just wow, I thought. They really were not as wise as I had thought.

The mental hospital is not a good place. It's mostly filled with people without homes. It smells bad, the food is terrible, and you are basically just locked up. If you're lucky, you get to talk to a doctor, who will just want to put you on meds. The doctors didn't like any of my answers. They didn't buy that I was having a spiritual emergency, an ascension. They didn't buy that I wasn't crazy. They wanted me to admit that I had bipolar disorder and to take the meds, which I refused.

I started feeling better the next day, again falling into a deep meditation while trying to ground myself. I still refused to be drugged by them. I wasn't going to take their drugs. I felt so much smarter than they all were. I was tapping into un-manifested energy—playing in the field of possibility. I hadn't quite learned this meant that you actually had to inhabit your body. I felt pulled away from this dimension, wanting to live in the one where peace, love, and oneness existed—a place of complete unconditional love and ultimate healing on all levels. I just knew it was possible. I just knew. But not there, not in the third dimension, the one filled with fear, pain, and suffering.

Shaking my head and almost laughing out loud at myself, I could hear my mom say again, "You came bareass naked, you can leave bareass naked." Which was how I had basically arrived this time at the loon. One of the nurses took me to the lost and found to find something to wear, as I only had the hospital gown I came in and nothing else. More irony, as I owned a clothing boutique filled to the brim with beautiful things but had to rummage through homeless people's old clothes for something to wear.

The only things I found that would fit were some green scrubs for pants and a burgundy zip-up hoodie with cream Sherpa trim on the hood and around the cuffs. It was balled-up and nasty. I put them in the wash, and that's what I wore for my three-day stay. I wasn't happy this time—I wasn't in my essence. There were no guides, no visitors, no friends to break me out and take me to Jake's restaurant for lunch and cocktails, like my friends Angi and Ali did last time.

This time I vowed to stay asleep.

No one wanted to hear my stories or participate in discussing my philosophies about life. Nobody cared of the rippling effect of mirror images reflecting back only endless perfection. There was no such thing as bad or good, life just is—an interaction of learning.

We are just here to experience it through our own selves, as our "Self."

Nobody wanted to hear it. No one wanted to talk about our connection, our oneness, our unlimited potential, healing, and amazing possibilities. Waking up this fast wasn't a good idea. I thought it was called ascension; I knew I wasn't bipolar. Wasn't this the whole entire reason for practicing all the fucking yoga and studying the sacred texts? To become enlightened? To have samadhi? Oh nope, it was only theoretical, apparently. Not something to be attained, especially not here—not in the West. Had this happened to me while living in an indigenous culture, I might have been watched over while on my spiritual journey, revered even. I might have been looked upon as one who could travel outside of their body to other dimensions.

On the shaman's journey.

But that's not what happened to me. My spiritual teacher and two of my most trusted, evolved friends had just dropped my ass off at the loony bin—again. Hadn't they known how hard this was on my girls and myself the first time, three years earlier? Couldn't they just take me back to my apartment, or even to a hotel? Nothing good happened at the loony bin. This had already taken such a negative toll on my life. I really wasn't sure how I would I survive this one or how I would convince my kids that I wasn't crazy again.

I would just stop. Just shut up. That's what I would do.

Why had it taken me so long to do this? Once again, all I needed to do was sweep all my feelings into just one or two words. Minimize my feelings so that they were easy to absolve, easy to wrap my head around—and then let them go.

"Shut Up!" I said it again out loud, to try it on and make it so. It was a phrase my grampa had said was ugly and rude, and he had asked me to please not say it when I was a young girl. But now it felt so right. "Kami, just shut up. Obviously, nobody cares!"

I would just shut up. Shut the fuck up.

And so, I did.

After my three-day hold, I was discharged. I called a cab and left the mental hospital barefoot, wearing the green scrubs and the ugly sweatshirt. I asked the cab driver to wait while I ran into the house to grab some money from my secret stash.

It was over $100 for the ride home. I didn't care; however, I should have as my finances were running very thin. My business was getting worse by the day. The rumors of my bipolar disorder and unusual behavior were swirling around my small town. I had missed Savvy's talent show—of course, these small things were a big deal to my kids, and needless to say, they were not happy with me and had become even more afraid of me.

My kids started becoming more and more distant after this trip to the mental hospital. Could you blame them though? Linda tried to lie to them about what was going on this time. She said that I was fine and told them they should just spend the night with her, as Dave was also in the hospital, having bicep surgery. It was too late for the lie, and it backfired. My girls saw right through it, discrediting me even more. This drove not just a wedge but a fucking football-stadium-sized wedge between me and my girls. I realized I needed to learn how to behave, to fit in, to be part of this 3D reality others called life.

This time, I would drop these two friends.

My grand plan was to shut up and pull myself together. I stopped all my spiritual studies and quit my twenty-year yoga practice. I stopped studying, walking, meditating, and researching. Everyone thought I was crazy, and I was tired of hearing about it. I packed up my altars, candles, tarot cards, and deities. I would give up the spiritual practices that had become such a big part of my life.

Luckily, I still had Savannah in my life. Now ten, she was always such a sweet love, and we had always been so connected, but I knew she was afraid of me, and it was heartbreaking. Our bond had been broken. Sam, refusing to visit me, had given me an ultimatum. I needed to be on medication before she'd see me, so I tried it—who cared? I was already numb; I could not care. I started taking the lithium for bipolar disorder and the Klonopin for insomnia and anxiety, which, of course, I didn't mind help with. I would certainly need to be drugged to fit into this new reality.

My once great life was falling to shit.

I hung up the ugly burgundy sweatshirt—as a reminder to pull my shit together. I even color-coordinated it into my clothing collection. It stood out like a sore thumb. I needed to see it as a daily reminder to never get that far out of my body again. It was not safe, dancing between the worlds. I would try to welcome my new reality without the comforts of my spiritual practice. I would try my hardest to make the best of it, to prove I was grounded. I would learn to behave, to be "normal." I couldn't change what had happened—it was too late for that. It didn't matter; drugs or no drugs, there was no convincing Sam that I was fine. She still refused to come to my house, and it crushed me.

PART FOUR

19

THE LAST VISIT WITH MY MOTHER

NOVEMBER 2013

My mother had not been doing well. She had been diagnosed with stage four lung cancer, and it was really just a matter of time. Her lifelong cigarette addiction had finally come to collect. Of course, she had quit when Sam was diagnosed with leukemia, making it all about herself, as always.

"My poor granddaughter has cancer, and here I am giving it to myself," she would say.

She had quit back then, but the damage had already been done. The chemo would keep her for a while, but it was just a matter of time. She had asked me to come to Utah for Thanksgiving, and so I did. I drove my little Kia from San Diego and stayed with a friend on the way. My friend had been struggling with family problems, and I didn't realize what I was walking into. It was a shit-show of a night at her house, and I hardly slept. I had planned to meet my mom for coffee.

After a twelve-hour drive to see her, I showed up fifteen minutes late, and she threw an absolute fit. Here she was, a grown-up, seventy-year-old woman, acting like a four-year-old child. There was no coffee for me.

"I have some Instant Folger's if you want." She knew I would turn my nose up at the offer, so she quickly added, "Besides, we need to go to the store to get the stuff you need for the pies."

It was the day before Thanksgiving, and she hadn't already bought ingredients for pies?

"Didn't you guys already go to the store?" I asked in disbelief. Of course, we couldn't go to just any store. She had to take me to a super fucking Walmart. She knew I hated Walmart. I have always disliked big box stores, and I have never liked grocery stores; it was hardly a secret. I had always felt they were full of subliminal messages, targeting us to spend money on the perfectly packaged poison and other crap they were serving up. I hated Walmart even more because of their known vendor relations—undercutting profits and crippling and taking out many small businesses not unlike my own.

This multi-billion-dollar company, like many others like them, has huge profits, yet their employees can barely make a living to support themselves.

Walmart was not a place I chose to support, but we went anyway. My mother was so mad, slamming the cart everywhere and basically leaving me in the giant store. Oddly enough, I ran into my brother-in-law, who helped me find my mom. Then she yelled at him because they were not coming for dinner that night.

"Donna, tomorrow is Thanksgiving, and we will be there all day," he said. I looked at him to save me, but I was on my own.

My mother didn't want to hear about my sadness, about my girls. Just like she didn't want to hear about the end of my marriage. While continuing to storm the aisles of Walmart, my mom asked, "Does he beat you? Does he cheat on you? Then why did you get divorced? Why did you get yourself into this mess? I think you two should just get back together." This from the woman who had been married six times! She would not let up on me, thinking she'd talk me into working it out with my husband. She had not heard anything I told her. Getting back together would be the answer to all my problems, she said. I should suck it up and get my life together. She had no idea that it was way too late for any of that, and she continued to go on and on about it. The damage was done; it was too late.

Thanksgiving was, surprisingly, quite lovely. My brother and sister were there. I loved them so much, but it always felt strained around my mother. Both were unsure who to defend, me or my mother. She always made them pick a side, and they always chose her, and I always felt like they were mad at me because of it. At Thanksgiving, I tried not to feel like a victim, but I couldn't help it. Once again, I wore the victimhood well.

My mom offered up some of her favorite porcelain dishes to me, wanting us to take a few sentimental items we might cherish, but, of course, she had to threaten me as she did.

"Don't sell those dishes, Kami!"

"Oh my God, Mom, can you give me a little credit? I am not going to sell these dishes!" I said.

It was a small set that included a vintage teapot and cups. It was something she knew I would love but that didn't have much value. We went through my mom's jewelry, some clothes, shoes, and makeup. She softened up, as she wanted to send some things with me to give to my girls. I found a few treasures that I wanted to take home for myself. I was thrilled to find my little, round Barbie suitcase, still filled with my original Barbie clothing collection. I also took a ton of fun costume jewelry from my great-aunt Jean and looked forward to sharing it with my girls.

I stayed with Keri that night and was hardly able to hold back the flood of ugly sobs that soon took over my entire body. My poor sister. She now looked at me wondering what to do to help. She listened intently while I grieved for my mother, grieved that she had never loved me. I knew it would be the last time I would see my mother, and deep down I really hated her. That's all I could say as I cried over my mother. "I hate her, I hate her, I hate her!"

Life for both of my siblings had not been entirely unlike mine. They'd both had a cross to bear growing up, and they both had paid their own fair price. Keri was the one person who had always looked up to me and admired me. I, of course, was always annoyed by it. I was five years older and probably jealous of her while growing up. She was the baby, and I felt as if she got all the attention and pampering. I used to call her Baby King Kong—when she was a toddler she would wander into our room and destroy hours of long work on my Barbie village, which was made out of all kinds of odd boxes and things I had structured together by gluing fabric to the sides to make wallpaper. I could work for hours designing Barbie houses and clothing. Now I felt bad for calling her that as I opened the treasured contents of my small Barbie suitcase and a flood of memories came back from my childhood. She had been a darling, little tow-headed toddler who grew into a super cute kid—skinny with straight, long blonde hair, perfect skin, and big blue eyes.

Keri was the only one who didn't leave home early; she never had the choice as my mom remarried and moved away, leaving my sister to finish up high school while living with our aunt Jolene. Keri went on to marry a great guy, Mike, and settle down in Cache Valley, the same town our mother lived in. Keri, too, bore the pain from children, unable to have any of her own. She adopted a baby and raised her as she would have her very own. My sister was born to be a mother. She was good at it, always babysitting every kid in town. She had grown up loving kids, and it was heartbreaking she couldn't have any of her own. This may have made her a soft mother, and her daughter became a challenge, taking the road of self-destruction as a teenager. Keri had a strong faith and felt blessed to be a mother, determined to overcome life's obstacles. She now enjoys a great life as a hairstylist and business owner of a hair salon.

My older brother, Mike, had also gotten married and had a few amazing kids; however, he, too, got lost in early adulthood, giving all his attention to drugs and selling them. He ended up without his wife, and, like me, had a severed relationship with his children. Unfortunately, he had to endure a not-so-pleasant life behind bars for five long years. Now remarried and quite successful in his trade working for the railroad, he is one of the biggest-hearted, hardest- working men I have ever met. He also turned his childhood love of trains into a lucrative career. Only now, instead of laying railroad track in our living room, he is in charge of bidding giant contracts and building the track for a large company. He followed in the footsteps of our maternal grandfather, who also worked for the railroad.

My brother and I, however, had a different kind of bond. I looked up to him and admired him like no other. When not even a teen himself, my brother broke up one of the many violent fights between my parents. I think I was maybe eight years old. Mike could hear the fighting from downstairs and came upstairs to my room to check on me and see what was going on. I was crouched on the floor in the corner by my Barbie village, crying while listening to my parents fight. He also checked on Keri, who I shared a room with—she was asleep in her crib. Then he sat on the floor and hugged me (something he never did) as we both sat and listened to our parents fight. The fight had escalated. My dad had a gun, and he was threatening to kill himself. Mike jumped up to leave my room and break up the fight, easily risking his own life. Our dad was over six feet tall and two hundred pounds—he was not someone to mess with, especially with a pistol in his hand. The rest of the night is a blur to my memory, but it was likely followed by a few days staying at my aunt Jolene's house. This intervention took its toll on the relationship Mike had with our dad, Greg. When Mike was in high school, he intervened again, accusing our father of having an affair with one of my mom's friends. My dad beat him up pretty badly, throwing him down the stairs and giving him two black eyes.

Violence was not a stranger in our house.

Was it the trauma that made up this deep connection between my siblings and me? We didn't talk all the time—and never discussed those dark moments from the past—but we had a strong bond, nonetheless. I felt that the tension between my mother and I came between us.

At Thanksgiving, everyone put their feelings aside and really showed up for my mother. I knew it would be the last time I would see her, and I think she knew it too. Maybe that's why she was so mean to me with her passive aggressive digs. She knew I would not show up and sit at her bedside and watch her die. She didn't want me to any more than I wanted to. She thought I had thrown my life away, that I had become a loser. She didn't say it, but she didn't need to. Her actions towards me said it all. She'd always had a condescending way of talking to me. She put me down for not being in Utah, for not being married, for not having my kids with me, for not curling my hair, or for not wanting to put on makeup. With my mother, everything had to be a certain way. I always felt her love came with conditions, many of which I refused to deliver. Wow, I thought, they were not unlike those of my husband.

The patterns really do repeat themselves. Without resolving the trauma, we often become exactly who we vowed not to.

20

BLACK FRIDAY

The next day, I got up early as I couldn't sleep. Even though I was emotionally exhausted, I wanted to get started on the long drive home. I needed to see my babies. It was Black Friday, a day I'd always despised. It always amazed me that Americans were so materialistic. After only one day of being grateful for everything they had, they would get up before the crack of dawn to literally trample over people for a good bargain.

But that day, I hardly cared about any of that. I cried almost all the way home from Utah. I had plenty of time, as the drive from Northern Utah to San Diego is quite a hike. As I had promised my mom, though, I called my aunt Jean. I thanked her for the costume jewelry and tried not to talk about my children and my heavy heart. Having no children of her own, she told me of the great connection she'd always had with my mom and of the lovely conversations that she looked forward to weekly. She just loved my mom and went on and on about her. That was the thing about my mom—everyone loved her but me. My mother would do anything for anybody, it felt like, except for me. She especially loved Aunt Jean, who lived in Napa, and who I had never met.

Aunt Jean and I enjoyed our fun, lighthearted conversation as I drove home. We talked of jewelry and fashion and how Aunt Jean used to dress up in the "good ol' days," wearing hats with matching gloves and pretty shoes. Ah, how I wished I had grown up in that era—so sophisticated. Aunt Jean told me she'd tell my mom to make sure I got enough of her inheritance for "an outfit or two!" I laughed at this, since Mom had always talked about the promise of her inheritance, always wishing to be rich. My aunt Jean was sweet and funny, it was easy to talk to her. I only wish I could have had this sort of connection with my mom. I told Jean of the fun costume jewels of hers that I would share with my girls. This made her happy to hear. I said goodbye, and I continued my drive back to San Diego.

As I got closer to home, I kept calling the girls. I was hoping to have dinner with them. They were both now living with their dad, but I still tried to make plans to see them. They were acting weird in their texts and wouldn't commit to dinner. I hadn't seen them in a week, and I really longed to catch up with them.

I drove into town and decided to stop by my ex's house to at least see the girls and deliver the many gifts and treasures from Aunt Jean and my mom. Sam had sent me a text that they were going to their dad's boat, so I thought I would find them at the house before they left. After the divorce, my ex bought a huge yacht that had two state rooms, a full kitchen, and a living room. It was nicer than any of the apartments I rented. I had spent my money from the sale of our house to pay off the huge credit card debt left over from my business after the recession. I really hadn't been that much of a genius after all—bankruptcy would have been a better option. The funny me always jokingly asked the bank teller, "Is this the small business bailout line?" when going to the bank. The 2008 recession had also shown a great shift of money from the middle class to the uber rich, decimating many small business while huge corporations were easily bailed out.

When I arrived, it appeared they had already left for Dave's boat. It was common for me to go to Dave's house when he wasn't home. I had let myself in for years, often making breakfast or lunch for the girls at his house, sometimes tidying up their room or closet then taking them to school. Dave loved grocery shopping and always had a stocked fridge. All things considered, we'd had a fairly amicable divorce. Sometimes I also helped take care of the girls' new dog, Cleo, who I just loved and would stop by to take on walks.

So, I figured I'd just go in and leave a few of the treasures for the girls. As I walked to the house, I walked by Sam's car, a BMW. Dave had bought it for her and given it to her six months before her sixteenth birthday. This was another one of those "firsts" that I hadn't been involved in. Dave had given it to her almost a whole year ago, on Christmas. After spending that Christmas Eve and Christmas morning with the girls, he had dropped them off at my apartment to say, "Sorry, man, I have to come back and get the girls in an hour."

"An hour? I get them for one fucking hour on Christmas?" had been my retort.

"Sorry, my girlfriend is on her way, and we have something special planned."

I looked around at my house, the presents, food, and my boyfriend, Bill. Did he think *we* didn't have anything special planned for Christmas? He showed up an hour later with a BMW for Sam, something he knew I would not approve of. She wouldn't even turn sixteen until June, and now I was the asshole because I wanted to spend time with my children on Christmas? Sam was over the moon, of course. She could hardly contain her excitement and was mad at me for wanting her to stay and spend time with me. I couldn't keep the tears from falling. Dave had looked at my boyfriend and said, "Dude, did I do the wrong thing, buying her a car?"

I wondered what Dave was up to now. I walked by Sam's car, curiously peeking inside. On the front seat was her handbag, open with her wallet and money showing. I shook my head as I walked into the empty house.

Sam's keys were on her dresser, so I took them to get her handbag out of the car, where it could easily be stolen. Next to her keys was a Coachella bracelet—the ticket for a huge outdoor music festival. Who was she going with? Who'd bought her this expensive ticket? She was barely sixteen, and, of course, she had not discussed this with me. When I opened the car door, I saw a huge bong on the back seat. I mean, a two-foot-tall water bong—not something that was easy to hide.

Now I was spinning. What else was she hiding? Back to her room I went. I found several items of mine that she had taken without my permission. Since they were mine, I took them back. Mad that my kids were not with me, I didn't think about the repercussions and took her car keys, the water bong, and the Coachella ticket-bracelet.

I sent a text to Sam. "I have your things. I want to see you, and you need to come over and talk about these particular things with me."

I drove home and explained the whole thing to my boyfriend, who said that what I'd done was a terrible idea and retreated to the garage. Then, just fifteen minutes later, my ex showed up pounding on my front door. The girls were waiting in the car. He was screaming and threatening to have me arrested for grand theft auto for taking the car keys.

"You should come in, and we should talk about this," I said. He refused. He was pissed, and this man was someone you did not want to fuck with. Even my six-foot-two, Grand-Canyon river-guide boyfriend didn't want anything to do with this current shit-show.

"Call them," I said. "Call the police, I have nothing to hide."

It was only a matter of minutes before one cop showed up, and then another. I stood with Samantha outside as the second cop showed up and asked us how things were while my ex talked with the other officer.

"Well, will you please tell my daughter what you will do if you pull her over and find her with marijuana and a giant water bong?" I asked the officer, cannabis not even being quite legal in California in 2013.

"You would lose your license until you were twenty-five," he said, wanting to clear this all up and go about his night.

I, of course, wouldn't hand over the bong or the buds, not wanting to get my kid in real trouble with the police. I handed over her empty bag to the cop, with no pot. I just wanted her to know the repercussions, to learn a lesson. I hadn't been the one who'd called the police, after all. I had to give back what I had "stolen." The officer convinced me to hand over the keys and the Coachella ticket to Sam, then both girls screamed at me as they got in the car with Dave.

"I fucking hate you! I hate you! I would rather kill myself than live with you," yelled Savannah.

I didn't even know how to respond to such words as they cut me to the core. I also realized they were not unlike what I had just said about my own mother.

They drove off, leaving Cleo, the darling, black half pug, half Boston terrier with me. I wasn't sure if they'd just forgotten her, but I welcomed the companionship.

21

RESTRAINING ORDER

A few days later, while driving to L.A. for work, I got a call from my boyfriend.

"Are you driving?" he asked. I told him yes, wondering what kind of dumb question that was. Of course, I was driving, I hadn't been gone that long. He asked me to stop and pull over. He said he needed to talk to me; it was important.

"Now? Why do you need to talk to me now?" I was on my way to meet up with a professional photographer, model, and hair and makeup artist—which I had never had for my photoshoots for It's a luv thing.

"I am late," I said.

I had gone from having a boutique to a VW bus. People didn't understand the mobile business I was launching, and my skin wasn't thick enough for all the questions that went along with doing something first. I had become less and less motivated to sell a dress or a T-shirt. But one of my friends, Wendy, saw the spark in me, and she knew I could do it. She was determined to help me get out of my funk. She was a hair and makeup artist and had a fancy photographer friend and a gorgeous model. I just needed to up my game. We had been planning this holiday photo shoot for weeks.

"This is important," Bill said again. "And I really need you to pull over for a few minutes, please." So I pulled over.

"What's up?" I asked, with serious irritation.

"Someone from the San Diego Sheriff's Department is here, and they would like to talk to you."

I sat in disbelief, in my car on some random exit off the I-5 freeway on my way to L.A., as the man from the Sherriff's Department spoke.

"Hello, hello, Ms. . . . Whaw, Whaw, Wha, wha . . . Wha, wha wha . . .." That was all I really heard—the sound the teacher makes on the Peanuts cartoon when Charlie Brown asks a question.

That's what it sounded like to me as I tried to get his words to sink in.

"Do you understand what I am saying?" he repeated, probably knowing I couldn't really comprehend what he was saying. My brain was completely unable to wrap itself around such a thing.

Once again, he repeated himself.

"If you call, text, or try to see your children in any way, you can and will be arrested. You are not allowed to come within one hundred feet of your children's schools, or your ex-husband's house. Do you understand? I am leaving this order from the court here at your house—there is a court date listed, and you will be expected to show up."

The court date was three months away. They were ordering me not to be a part of my children's lives for at least three months. I was being served a restraining order for trying to be a good and involved parent. Or so I thought. This restraining order might as well have been a death sentence.

I had certainly been served.

22
ROT IN HELL

I walked out of the courtroom, head held high as I tried to calm myself from the rage that was stewing inside. I tried hard to choke back the intense pain searing through my heart and bubbling its way to the surface. Ahead of me was the man who took away my children. Despite his perfectly pressed, grey Glen plaid suit and crisp white shirt, I could still see and sense his fear. He was afraid of me. He walked up to the bailiff, asking to be escorted with his attorney from the courtroom. What a pussy, I thought, as I glared at this man, who was once my husband. He might as well have been a complete stranger. I was glad he could feel my energy as I walked behind him and his frumpy, grey-haired lady attorney. It was a long walk down the narrow hall from courtroom number four. He felt me behind him, and I didn't back off. He had declared I was crazy, and now my kids were gone, so what did I have left?

You want crazy? I'll show you fucking crazy! Take away any mother's children, and what you'll have left is certainly the definition of crazy. He stopped at the drinking fountain, pretending to get water so that I would pass him. He felt me and knew to get out of my way. I passed him, trying hard to hold my inner self together. I barely made it into the bathroom before the tears started, followed by a horrible shrill sound that came from deep inside my chest. The quiet yet pitiful cry that I had been holding in during court finally made its way out like vile vomit, as I shut the stall door and fell to the floor. It was a deep wailing kind of cry full of disbelief and sadness. My body shook and I began to sweat while crying out for my babies. Even though they were now fourteen and sixteen, they were still my babies. I missed them so much.

My family was convinced I was crazy, or psycho, as Savvy's attorney had told the courtroom. Court had not gone well and certainly not in my favor. I was unable to afford an attorney and instead showed up talking like the broken crazy woman Dave had portrayed to the court. The judge was also kind enough to point out that I was an unfit mother, seeing as how I could not financially support my children. All kinds of other stupid shit had been brought up at court. Apparently, my lack of a poison-filled pantry—poison that some called food—further confirmed my inability to be a good mother. It didn't matter that I cared to have fresh food rather than the packaged food most people deemed as food for dinner. I guess having those items meant you were being a good, responsible parent. I had not stocked up on such commodities because I knew they were unhealthy. Were we really wasting the court's time, talking about what kind of food I did or didn't buy for my girls? Dave literally continued to air my dirty laundry by telling the courts that my children also went without having clean clothes at my place—the laundry, of course, not always being finished. The fucking laundry again! What a joke. I kept a fairly fucking tidy house, but there would be no convincing anyone of my homemaking abilities here. It did not matter. And then Dave brought up the marijuana, really?

The court made sure to make note of my irresponsible behavior—smoking pot—even though I had a medical license, and, of course, my recent DUI, which further confirmed what a horrible person I was. It didn't matter that I had been pulled over for talking on the phone after having drunk only one glass of wine. It also didn't matter that I had been the bread winner for most of our marriage and that I'd already had to pay Dave in order to get a divorce. Of course, now none of that mattered. I was unable to financially support my children without a full-time job, and I lost because of it.

I was forced to give up custody of my children in order to remove the restraining order; there would be no winning in this battle. My ex had drawn the line this time, and there would be no crossing it. I had lost them.

How could I possibly live life without my children? How would they go through teenage life—puberty, boys, school, dances, and friends—without their mother, and why would they want to? Try as I might, my mind just couldn't wrap itself around this one. "She will not honor their wishes," Dave had said many times. I was not trying to honor their wishes; I was trying to raise good humans! And most good parents know teenagers are not ready to make all the best decisions for themselves, but my own didn't like my way of parenting or the rules I required them to follow. They preferred Dave's house, where they could stay up late at night and do as they pleased. I was tough and could withstand obstacles. I'd had a few curve balls thrown my way, but dealing with the unexpected loss of my children was definitely not in any of my playbooks. I was done, defeated, and broken.

I tried to collect myself as I left the courthouse and walked down the street to Starbucks, where my friend Marci was picking me up. Despite my perfect hair, makeup, and borrowed black wrap dress, I was a complete wreck. My acrylic-heeled, strappy sandals smacked on the concrete as I continued to sob and walk down the street from the courthouse. A cute guy in his early twenties stopped and rolled down his window.

"Are you okay?" he asked.

"NO! I am NOT okay!" was my swift response.

I probably scared the hell out of that poor bastard too. My children had been taken away and turned against me. I watched in the parking lot as my once-husband pretended to laugh while conversing with his attorney. He could honestly manipulate a telephone pole he was so good, and he had taught this skill to our oldest daughter—he just couldn't see it yet.

I stood there on the corner by the Starbucks, waiting for him to pass by in his car. I had already been called crazy, so what did it matter—what was the point?

So that is what I did. I stood on the corner like a crazy person, and I pointed right at him. I stood by the busy street by the courthouse in my high heels and black dress—and with tears, lots of them, rolling uncontrollably down my face, I pointed while I screamed, "You will rot in hell! You will rot in hell! You will rot in hell!" I pointed and yelled at him while he sat at the light in his smug, little blue Prius. The look of pity on his face will be engrained in my mind forever.

My usual talk of forgiveness had totally fled. Mama bear was now out in full fucking force, and if you have ever crossed a mama bear, you know of her wrath.

Today was May 19, the birthday of both my boyfriend and my biological father. Where were these two men? Not there when I needed them, that was for sure. What had happened to my life? I had asked the question so many times. I had really thought I was on a spiritual journey—well this was one fucking journey I didn't want to be on. I'd always thought I had ascended too quickly, but I was done. I had quit. I thought I had gotten off the ride.

I no longer wanted to be on a spiritual journey. I didn't want to be a light-worker, an indigo, a Star-seed, a Bodhisattva, or a bipolar crazy person. None of these labels fit for me. I had often been called them long before I even knew what they meant. Most of those labels referred to being part of a spiritual awakening for the planet. But I didn't want to be associated with any of the labels or the awakening of the planet. I just wanted my kids back.

Hadn't I tried to get off the ride after my last trip to the loon? What the fuck? Somehow, I knew there was no getting off the ride, off the journey. Only through. But how I would get through this one? I really wasn't quite sure.

I was uncertain how I would find myself again this time. After arriving home from court that day, I could barely move, eat, sleep, or get out of bed. I certainly could not work. I could not put on a happy face and get excited about selling a stupid dress out of a VW bus. I hardly cared when a week later the notice came that my lease would not be renewed for my current apartment. I had loved the enchanting space overlooking Swami's Beach and the Self-Realization Fellowship center. I had spent countless hours in deep meditation there, loving the support and oneness that the serene temple provided, and now, that, too, would soon come to an end.

Now what?

I called a friend. It seemed I had very few left at this point. I timidly asked, "What has happened to my life? Honestly, tell me, how did I fuck it up so badly? Was this my spiritual path? Now my kids want me out of their lives, and soon I will have no place to live." I was hysterical and crying.

"You really need to see a psychiatrist, and you need to be on medication," she counseled. "And you need to stop smoking marijuana. And whatever you do, don't text your kids!" It was sound advice, but I didn't want to hear it.

I hung up on her, yelling in my mind, "Fuck you! Fuck you, fuck you! You try going months without seeing or talking to your kids and see how you feel!"

I shook my head at my own self, trying to remind myself that I could not blame others for my obstacles, but I hardly cared. I was walking a thin line of not wanting to be on this planet. I had recently pulled together my first funeral for a perfect lost soul. He was sensitive and sweet and clearly not like everyone else. He was like me though. His parents had asked me to befriend him. I had tried and obviously failed. Now I was painting and preparing an altar, ordering flowers, tables, and chairs for his family to come and mourn his precious being. Planning his funeral was the least I could do for the sweet soul who hadn't made it. Life in this reality is just too unbearable for some. I certainly understood.

This time even work couldn't save me. My depression ran too deep. Where would I run to this time? I had run away from home at seventeen, my mother yelling at me as I literally ran down the street. I had left behind my whole world and all the mementos of my cheerleading days: my boyfriend, best friends, dolls, trophies, vinyl records—and my prized, amazing light-up jukebox—all never to be seen again. I ran and never turned back. I had turned to drugs and alcohol, of course, even finding comfort in cocaine. It had been the eighties; cocaine had been pure and clean, and easy to come by.

But no drugs or alcohol could possibly numb this much pain. I hadn't seen my kids in almost seven months. I was broken, with no repair in sight.

The last time I had needed support in my life, I had turned to Nordstrom for solace. Back then Nordstrom was my home away from home—a perfect place in which to hide—and it had been a much better and more acceptable addiction. My addiction wasn't shopping, of course. It would have been, had I the pocketbook to support it, but those days were long gone. I just needed a job. I decided to pull myself together and call Nordstrom to see about getting an interview. Miraculously, I was able to schedule one. Now to just get a job.

Work was no longer my addiction of choice—Cannabis was. I had taken up smoking pot when I left Dave, trying to calm the anxiety and panic that overwhelmed me daily. I would often wake up in the night in a sweat, panicking as to how I might support myself and my children. Maybe I should have smoked more pot with Dave when we were married.

Back then, it had been his habit, and now it was mine. I now loved cannabis and smoked it daily as my only ritual. Even my kids knew. They must've told their father because now I was deemed the drug addict. My use of cannabis, not quite legal yet, had come up in court, and I was being judged because of it. I still couldn't believe it, thinking of Dave as I puffed on my own pipe. He was such a hypocrite. He'd been smoking pot since age thirteen, and even let the girls smoke it. Of all the things, cannabis was now being used against me.

A few months earlier when coming to pick up the girls from his house, I'd embarrassed him by asking, "Will the real pot smoker of the family please come forward?" in front of Sam, who knew I'd been smoking and was not happy about it.

He sheepishly said, "It's me."

Guilty as charged.

In court, I had admitted that I'd been using cannabis to cope with anxiety—and that I had a medical license to do so. Was that so wrong? To my mind, cannabis was far safer and better than any of the psychiatric drugs that they so freely gave out. It didn't matter; the court did not respond in my favor. I was deemed the bad person.

23

LOST BUT NOT FOUND

I lost myself at Nordstrom in Collectors, the high-end designer department. It really was a beautiful place to be lost, but boy did I feel like a fish out of water. I am hardly the designer type, but I didn't care. I needed a job. I needed to be able to show the courts and any future landlords that I was responsible and respectable. On my first day, I remerchandised the department, moving things around, and then got in trouble for it. I soon learned that certain designers do not like to be hung next to certain other designers. I didn't know that designers were that picky. Who knew Donna Karan and Pucci could not be friends? In this designer world, I felt such division and competition, unlike the family unity I had experienced in the men's division or in the surf industry.

Nicole, who had hired me that day long ago at the Brass Plum, now stepped onto the Collectors floor in La Jolla, almost thirty years later, to visit me. We hadn't seen one another for twenty years. Marriage, moving, change of names and phone numbers, and, of course, children had led us to different lives. But here we were, reunited once again through another mutual friend, Lynn, who had once been my boss while I worked for Nordstrom in Seattle. Now here Nicole was with her two beautiful children and her father. One daughter was spunky, like her mom, with golden-white hair just like Sam's. They were both amazing kids, with kind faces. Her father I remembered from long ago. Her mother, who had passed, had often sent us dried spaghetti in the mail, worried we were going to starve because we were so poor and hardly able to live on our meager $800-a-month salary.

Nicole laughed when she saw me, but not in a good way. "Here you are. Oh my—look how thin you are!" she said. I was forty-eight and barely pushing 105. I hadn't been that thin since I was a sophomore in high school.

"All those years of thinking yourself skinny before getting on the scale really does work!" I teased my longtime friend.

Nicole bowed her head, "I was so mean!"

"Well, you were a little mean, and I was a little chunky," I replied. Bulimia had been part of my addiction back then, but I hadn't mentioned it back then, or now.

"Hey, *The Secret*," her daughter chimed in.

Yes, the book called *The Secret*. I believed it was true that whatever we believed did in fact become our reality. Yes, I was thin, this was true, but my current reality was beyond painful, and I was in it. I was trying to go through the motions, trying to observe my life's movie and make changes without being attached. I realized we could never change the movie by changing the screen, you had to change your life—from the movie projector—from the inside.

This was *The Secret,* the real one.

However, my current projection was still a really bad movie. It was dark grey, with no color, no fun, and no laughing—just grey, like the smoke from my constant cannabis smoking those days. Mary Jane was my new and adored friend—maybe the only one. Weeks rolled by, and still I hadn't seen or heard from my children. I was worried about how they were doing, but I couldn't even text Dave to find out how they were.

One day after work, I met my friend Julie for a burger. Our youngest daughters were BFFs, and luckily, I knew she was keeping a good eye on my teenager. Her daughter had texted her that Savvy wasn't going home with her that day but was going on to another party and spending the night with some girl I didn't know. I asked Julie about the girl, and she didn't have to answer—the look on her face said it all. So their father didn't want me to parent our kids, but it was fine for them to be roaming the neighborhood and staying overnight at a stranger's house? Dave slept in the converted garage that was not even attached to the house where my teen girls currently resided, free to do whatever they wanted. All of this was fine with him—and apparently also with the courts. Dave, religiously asleep by 8:30 p.m., left my fourteen- and sixteen-year-old girls to do as they pleased. They had the house to themselves. A nightmare to me—but certainly a dream to my teens.

I was silent as I listened to Julie tell me of my daughter's whereabouts. Afterwards I walked to my car, the tears streaming down my face just like the rain that drizzled down from the grey sky. I started the car, and on the radio was Fleetwood Mac, singing, "You can go your own way." But I didn't want to go my own way. I wanted to take it all back, go back. I didn't want to go home, but I should have been more grateful—soon I would have no home at all.

Summer in my small beach town was the place to be, and everyone wanted in. Rental properties were being leased within an hour while forty people waited in line to apply. I'd seen twenty-seven properties, and even if I had made it to the top spot, with my horrible credit due to the IRS collection, my lack of cash, and lack of verified income, things were not looking favorable for me. My recent sanctuary working at Nordstrom had quickly turned south. The corporate mentality, or rather corporate slavery, in my opinion, had taken over my beloved Nord. The department manager was entitled, intimidating, and scary. What had happened? Maybe I had grown too carefree and easygoing for that uptight environment. It was hard for me to rally and sell after being called into the manager's office daily at the beginning of my shift to be told of my tedious wrongdoings the day before. I didn't like being in trouble, it blew my sales mojo and made me anxious. My paycheck for two weeks of almost full-time work was $600. Wow. Now I saw why the youth didn't want to work. I couldn't even have afforded a psychiatrist if I had wanted one. How were people surviving on $15 an hour in San Diego, which had one of the highest rents in Southern California? I didn't believe there had been a raise in commission for the salespeople since I'd left there twenty years ago.

We parted on fairly mutual terms, meaning they would find a better suited department for me, but they really wanted to fire me—I was hardly the model employee I had once been. I showed up late and was often unable to meet my daily sales quotas. I no longer had the drive or the passion for working for a big company that had once fueled me. As easy as I had come, I would also go. I would no longer hear that beep, beep, beep through the secure employee entrance or be part of a team that did everything together. I had done that already, and I was okay with it. I left, taking with me a few new friends and some interesting encounters from working with the high-end clientele in the Collectors department.

I bought a last pair of shoes with my discount and happily walked out the front doors, unfortunately leaving behind a spare pair of cobalt blue, brown, and orange shoes; just like me, they would go to the "lost and found," never to be picked up.

I walked out the doors for the last time, contemplating the fear that enveloped me. I wasn't sure I was smart enough or strong enough this time to get myself out. My worst fears had come to fruition, haunting me like a bad nightmare. I had lost my daughters and my job at Nordstrom, and I might soon be homeless. I really had no other choice than to stare fear fully in the face.

What would I do now?

I wasn't the only one to have recently walked out the door. I could still see Savannah in what seemed like a bad dream, walking down the stairs and out the door months ago. The enormity of my girls not wanting to be with me was just a burden too big to bear. The life I was living really was a nightmare, and somehow, I had created it.

I only wished that it was a dream I could wake up from. It had already been eight months since Savvy, my heart of hearts, had left one Saturday morning—I could still vividly see her determined face and stern eyes, her ponytail swinging as she walked out the door.

This event had been just before the restraining order incident. Savannah and I were going to walk to breakfast together at Swami's Cafe, which we both loved. I was content, happy even. It was a beautiful day out, and I was looking forward to spending the day with my baby girl. She was upstairs getting ready, and I was unloading the dishwasher. There was a loud knock at the door. It was Dave, and before I even realized what was happening, down the steps she flew with her bag slung over her shoulder, and just like that, she was gone. She shot me a look, and it reminded me of myself when I ran away at age seventeen. Just like me, she didn't bother to look back as her bulldog daddy held guard at the door. My youngest daughter had walked out of my apartment at age fourteen, the same age as her sister when she had refused to live with me. She, too, would never come back.

I had not honored her wishes and taken her to her dad's the night before. He had told me he wasn't feeling well, so I'd said she should just come to my house. Just like that, she was done with me. She and my ex-husband decided she would also live with him. Sam had come less and less over the years, and now Savvy wanted to live with her dad full-time. Regardless of the custody laws, my children and Dave would always just do what they wanted. "They are old enough to choose," was his response. Why choose to live with your mom, where there were rules and discipline, when you could live with your dad and do what you wanted? Not to mention that he was always happy to pick up the bill for whatever they might want, happy to buy and pay for their love. It had worked. He wasn't intentional about his manipulation—it was just who he was; he just didn't see it as a bad thing. He was a good dad, and the girls could depend on him—for that I was grateful.

I looked around at her room as I packed up the contents of my apartment overlooking Swami's Beach to put my life in storage. All I could find or afford was a temporary room for a month from a spiritual sister in the community. My friends had dwindled, my career was in the toilet, but my biggest heartache was that my kids were still not speaking to me, creating a pain so severe it immobilized me. Somehow, I couch-surfed at friends, stayed with lovers and customers, and—when I could afford it—the Motel 6. Jobless, homeless, and kidless, I had nothing more to fear, so fear and I made friends, at least for the time being.

24
CITY OF LOST ANGELS

A few months later, I went shopping in the Fashion District in downtown L.A.—something I had done almost weekly for the past nine years but not anymore. I always felt so inspired and alive in L.A. Unfortunately, this time I was only shopping for a few special orders for a handful of It's a luv thing customers. That was all I could afford to invest. I was about finished—it was the end of the road for my business. I had tried over the previous few months to keep it afloat while also working at Nordstrom, but the end had been just around the corner for my Luv thing, and I felt it.

I looked up as I passed the Citadel, an outlet store that was the last chance for most of the inventory sold there. I was reflecting on the end of the road. I had such an eerie feeling this time when I passed. The giant statues made me feel as though I were crossing into the promised land. I laughed and thought, "Oh, how I only wish it were so." I was on my way to visit a new spiritual sister friend in a tiny gem of a town called Cheviot Hills. Even the name sounded glamourous— tucked away in the City of Lost Angels. That was what I and others often called the city, so overflowing with money and poverty, both in the same place, that it was easy to become a lost soul there. I loved the dichotomy, the aliveness that the city exuded. L.A. was a great place to be lost. I'd had a couple of friends and a few lovers in this city. I also had a lot more good memories than I did bad ones. After I finished shopping, I headed north to say hello to Alesha. The minute I walked up her steps, I said, "This place is so cute I wish I lived here."

Without really looking up, she said, "Great, you can, because I am moving out tomorrow!"

"Perfect! I will unpack the shit out of my car!" And so, I did, both of us laughing at our funny greeting—she moved out and I moved in. Just like that. It was month-to-month and included a very part-time job to help pay for the very affordable rent. I felt such gratitude.

I rooted in as I unpacked the few things from the car, and really felt okay for the first time in a while. My body was exhausted from the stress of worrying about how I was going to support myself, get myself financially on my feet, and renew my relationship with my children. It was a lot, not to mention the added strain of wondering where I might lay my head each night. Since the six-month restraining order had been lifted, I had been sending my children daily texts. I then started leaving nice voice-mail messages. I thought it would be good for them to hear my voice. I unpacked and tidied up, enjoying the new space with an outdoor living room and a perfect, manicured lawn. The lovely, little stucco homes with red-shingled roofs put a smile on my face as I cruised down the streets to check out my new neighborhood. I had been there only two days, and already I felt the layers of tension sloughing off. I felt more alive and more in tune with myself, letting go of just a little of the panic state that had become my recent everyday norm.

I sorted through my endless daily emails—delete, delete— then ouch, another stab to the heart. The court was saying that the girls "preferred that I text them only." Then I opened an email stating that if I continued to call my children on the phone, I could be held in contempt of court or possibly thrown in jail. Wow, good thing I did not notify anybody of my new address. I wouldn't want the San Diego sheriff to drive all the way to L.A. just to arrest a woman for calling her children. I laughed, and tears once again streamed down my face. Was I such a horrible person, that I should not be allowed to call my own children?

Was I a horrible person because I went down my spiritual path, or maybe just a little too far down the rabbit hole? Once you went down the rabbit hole of truth it was hard to un-see the truth and to not want to share it.

Or was it because I was a creative, passionate person who occasionally got mad and yelled at my kids? Hadn't all mothers yelled at their kids? Did my short temper make me a terrible mother? Did that deem a mother crazy and unfit? I had thought it meant I really cared. Had I not cared, why would I have even bothered being mad? And because I didn't keep a pantry stocked full of junk food, I was not feeding them, according to my husband's lawyer. Talk about crazy—the world really was upside down.

I had sold my VW bus, put all my stuff in storage, and settled into the tiny furnished studio apartment in Cheviot Hills. I didn't mind taking over a few odd jobs assisting with some workshops for the man who lived in the front house in exchange for most of the rent. I also somehow managed to get a job working for a staging company in L.A. It was a great way to really get to know L.A. and to lose myself in a new creative outlet, and it took my mind off my hideous life. I welcomed the distraction of learning something new. I had always been intrigued by interior design and didn't mind the hard work that came with pulling it all together. But I sure didn't love the ridiculous daily traffic. Getting anywhere in the city took at least half an hour—if you were lucky. Making friends in Los Angeles was not easy, which probably had something to do with the broken demeanor I carried with me everywhere.

The job, the temporary L.A. sanctuary, and my small amount of money were all short-lived. Just like that, they all seemed to fizzle out as fast as they came. This time I got fired for changing out the lamp shades from black to white at a client's request. Customer service had been instilled in me from my days at Nordstrom. I had agreed with her—the black shades stood out like a sore thumb in the posh condo with all-white interior in Santa Monica. Customer service, however, was not a priority at the staging company—breaking up a furniture collection was taboo. I didn't even bother to go back; I knew I was fired. They sent me a text to come pick up my check. The next week my landlord said he had been notified by the homeowner that he could no longer sublet the studio, and that was pretty much it for my L.A. life, and it had only been a few months.

Life was harsh, and at the end of the day, I was still stuck with me—spiritual, bipolar—whatever you wanted to label me. If I had any angels out there looking over me, I prayed, really prayed they would look after me. I spent that birthday alone, curled up on the red outdoor sofa sheltered by a wooden awning with sprawling vines that ran down the sides. The tears on my face fell silently, just like the rain.

25

SEATTLE BLUES

Once again, there was nowhere to go. I was homeless over the holidays, thankful to take an unpaid housesitting job for a friend. That Christmas was one of the saddest to date, as I spent the day watching the cat chase a rat in the big yard where I had helped with the funeral services. The only gift given or received that year was a CD of the Blind Boys of Alabama from Goldy, who owned the home and had produced the album, which I listened to nonstop. If those blind men could sing about seeing the light and finding Jesus, I could too, right? I had given up on most of my prayers, but maybe, just maybe, that was exactly what I needed. So, I got right down on my knees in my friend's big yard and prayed, as I wondered who would invite me to "sit at the welcome table" that those beautiful men sang about. I only wished I felt more welcome, or that I had a table to sit at as I tried hard to find some gratitude.

It was also in this big yard that I had met Anne. The shaman I'd been working with said I needed to find my spiritual grandmother, that she had a gift for me. Goldy's mother had assisted Anne throughout the years on her spiritual endeavors. Anne was the first White woman to have been initiated into a revered circle of Native American women. She had risen to the top of the clan, becoming their leader. Anne had shown up several times at holidays at my friend's house and had given me well-needed spiritual advice more than once.

I had made an appointment to meet Anne. She told me she felt lost and sad that she had not completed her journey of bringing light, truth, and goodness to the planet. Her tribe had been practicing rituals and storytelling for decades.

At the end of the meeting, I asked her spiritual name and if she had something to pass down to me.

"Rainbow Dragonfly," was her response.

I jumped up and started skipping around her in delight. I was part of the rainbow tribe, I told her. The century-long prophecy would be upheld, I was sure of it! I would do my best to hold the torch or pass the peace pipe, I said, laughing. Anne's clan were called the "pipe carriers," but they didn't actually smoke the pipes, not that I knew of. They all had beautiful, ornate pipes, which they used in ceremony to call in the elements—spirit guides as well as the four directions. Anne wanted to have a pipe made for me. I laughed as I assured her I was an excellent pipe maker, preferring to smoke from a homemade apple pipe. I was elated we both held the same vision for the planet, the vision of the rainbow people.

The short story of the rainbow tribe is that the Native people were told that the White people would come and decimate their land, taking everything from them. After seven generations (the seven fires), all people would come to a fork in the road. They would either choose the path of materialism, which is led by power and fear, or choose the path of spirituality, love, and living in unison with the planet. People of all colors would come together to restore balance to the planet with love and compassion—they would be the awakened ones. These were the rainbow warriors. I knew I was part of this tribe, even if I hadn't met any of them yet.

Magically, shortly after Christmas, my old Nordstrom buying buddy, Nikki, helped me land a job at Nolily, an off-priced company based in Seattle, where she was currently working. They even offered to pay for me to move there. I was relieved after being fairly homeless and unsettled for a large part of last year. Now I could get my stuff out of storage and finally breathe, well, kind of. The broken heart over the loss of my children had left me only a shell of a person. Moving away was just what I needed. I could hardly bear to be in my small beach town, where I knew everyone and the first question asked always sent a knife through my heart. "Hi, how are you? How are your girls?"

This simple, polite question was more than I could handle.

It was late January when I loaded my tiny Kia and drove away, barely looking back as I headed up the coast of California, back to the city of grey and rain. I welcomed it with open arms though. I joked that if you were going to be depressed, you might as well live in a depressing city. Seattle could certainly put out that vibe, with its constant, grey drizzle.

I had a few weeks before my job would start, so I checked into a hotel that my new company had provided while I looked for a place to live. My stepdad, Greg, and his wife wired me the funds for the first month's rent and deposit. It was a loan—more money than I'd had in years, and I graciously accepted. Finding a place to live was not that easy, and I ended up choosing a new high-rise apartment with a rooftop deck that sat right under the Space Needle. I was thrilled to get lost in this city where nobody knew me, and I felt the layers of financial stress peel away. I spent hours gazing at the Space Needle from the rooftop or roaming the city through the sculpture park, the wharf, and Pike Place Market. Sometimes I would stop at a favorite local bar or restaurant, then ride the monorail back to Queen Anne. I loved the city, but unfortunately, I hated the job. I hated the way everyone was so phony and the ridiculous business plan, where they offered the vendors extremely low margins but Nolily owned nothing themselves. All the risk was on the vendor; there was no buying accountability, whatsoever. Unlike the high standards that were expected at Nordstrom, Nolily employed a bunch of overpaid buyer wannabes who bought nothing, as Nolily held no inventory and only purchased the off-price goods from the vendor after they were sold. In fact, I hated everything about it, except for the money.

Maybe I just hated myself, I thought. After three short months, they sold the company, and the downsizing happened fast. My boss couldn't wait to fire me—she had told me I needed to "filter" myself. My problem was that I spoke my mind and said what I thought. I no longer cared to drink the Kool-Aid or kiss ass, and this did not bode well with my boss. She said I wasn't a team player.

The day she fired me, I walked home, anxious as I hurried to check my stash of sleeping pills to see how many there were. I was unsure if the small amount I'd saved up would even be enough to do the job, but just knowing I had them made me feel better. I planned it out in my head, just in case—just in case.

I had only been in Seattle a few months. I had practically just arrived, and I had already lost my job. Fired. Escorted out—bag packed and handed to me. Yep, on the Friday afternoon before Mother's Day, and if you knew me, you would know. I Fucking Hate Mother's Day! Yep, and I hate the word *hate*—and *stupid* and *kill*. They were terrible words that I didn't allow my children to use, but I also hated this day. This was a first for me, and it hit me like a ton of bricks. Work was the one thing I was always really good at, or so I had thought.

Now what? I had just arrived there, and I owed so much money to so many people. I was in a lease in a new apartment in downtown Seattle, and I had zero savings—nothing. I had really been banking on this new job to get me on my feet.

The next day, when I called my mom, I told her I wanted to join an ashram.

"What's an ashram?" she asked.

"Just a place in India you join to devote your life to meditation and prayer," I answered.

"I'm just sure you're not going to do that!" she responded.

This was something she said about everything I did. She had said it about my moving to Idaho, to Seattle that first time, to Alaska—even to California. Even now, she couldn't understand why I didn't want to be in Utah with my family.

"What's wrong with joining an ashram?" I asked. "It's simply a place where you can have respite, a silent retreat to meditate for hours a day, giving yourself to God. Why not?"

She could not wrap her head around that idea at all.

I shot back with, "Well, it is certainly better than the alternative!"

I shouldn't have said that, because then she started screaming at me. "I can't talk to you. I can't deal with you!" And then she hung up. Why was I surprised that there was no compassion or concern for me and my well-being?

A few minutes later, my phone rang again. It was my brother.

"Mom called and said you're going to kill yourself! What the fuck is wrong with you? Mom has cancer, and you tell her you are going to kill yourself on Mother's Day!"

I hadn't actually said that, had I? Why was I even bothering to talk to her? Hadn't I told myself I was done with her last year when she thought I might sell her old dishes? I'd honestly thought she cared more about what I might do with the fucking dishes than she did about me.

Who would really give a shit anyway?

26

DESIGNING MY WAY OUT OF DEPRESSION

JUNE 2015

After being fired from Nolily, I wallowed, cried, and wallowed and cried some more. Then once again, Nicoli Leonard came to the rescue. Seattle was her hometown, and she had moved back with her husband, who was a store manager at Nordstrom. She had settled in and was now selling real estate. She took me on a few realtor tours, and I soon found a staging company I wanted to work for. I called them up, determined to get a job. I offered a day of design work for free. It had worked last time, so I tried it again. Thankfully, I got the job and began working for them the next week.

Once again, I appreciated the hard work and creativity that the job demanded, but it was not easy. It was physically exhausting. Staging houses was just like moving, but all in one day, not leaving until everything was absolutely perfect—and we did it daily. I loved the excitement of waking up with just an address, often feeling like I was on some sort of scavenger hunt as I looked for the hidden key at the property to open the place I would design that day. Seattle was full of amazing architecture, and I looked forward to designing all the different styles of houses, turning them into darling, little, cozy homes that someone would want to buy. I preferred the old traditional Tudor-style houses with character and charm over the big-box style new houses that were sprinkled all over the East side. My favorite all-time house was a big historic Colonial on Capitol Hill. The place was enormous, with big, white columns on the front porch and four full floors. Instead of the two days we usually took to do a house, this one took me three full days. Every single detail was going to be left perfect. This house was such a fun challenge, with so many built-in shelves and alcoves, and I cherished every minute of it. I designed the entire home in pink and cream. It was absolutely elegant and stunning. I filled the home with old-world overstuffed furniture. I especially loved the pink and cream herringbone chairs with ornate feet, which I featured on either side of the grand fireplace. I imagined what it would be like to live in such a grand home with laughing children running up and down the stairs. It even had a hidden back stairway, probably once used for servants. I wondered what those walls would say if they could talk.

Dreaming and designing homes kept my mind and days busy and kept me from wanting to think about my own life, or lack thereof. There were five or six designers at the big, swanky company I worked for, and we all fought to work on the mid-century modern homes with the clean lines and funky furniture. I loved the style from that era and dreamed of owning one myself someday. I dreamed of living in all of those homes, if only for a moment. I found joy in leaving everything impeccable. I found it rewarding at the end of the day, seeing it all come together somehow as if by magic. We even got to rent art from the Seattle Art Museum from time to time. Another Nicki would teach me the art of staging and design; we soon became fast friends, both sharing in our need for perfection. Nicki felt right at home at the SAM, and I loved going there with her. She had a knack for choosing the perfect art. It was such a treat to go there, picking out the all-important art then having it wrapped up to take to that day's installation.

The SAM. Even in Seattle, far away from her, I couldn't escape the heartbreak—I saw things everywhere that reminded me of my Sam. Wherever I went, there I was, sitting with my pain. If only I could have surrounded myself with enough beauty to soothe my open wounds. There just wasn't enough furniture, and there were not enough gorgeous homes big enough to fill that void. I certainly tried.

Seattle was a great place to be depressed. It was easy, welcoming even. It was easy to let the tears run down your face daily, like the daily drizzle of the rain. Nobody really noticed, and if they did, they wouldn't have said anything. I got my daily dose of entertainment watching the bus stop below through the window and seeing everyone going on about their day with their heads down like ants—dressed in black head to toe—the uniform of most Seattle peeps. Once again, I managed to find the best apartment ever. It fit me better, anyway, than the high-rise apartment. It was a 1920s walk-up in Lower Queen Anne. Of course, I swooned over the architecture, with its quaint, old-style kitchen and stove, and a window where I could still spend countless hours looking out at the Space Needle, just blocks away. I sent my prayers there, straight up to the tallest point to the sky.

Praying was something I still did, almost unconsciously. I felt as though talking to God was the only thing I did, while talking to people was something I did less and less of. I lived alone, mostly worked alone, and spent most days all alone with my depression. I had decided to splurge, though, as I'd made plans with my best friend, Dodo, who still lived in Seattle, to meet for a manicure and lunch. She was busy working at what I had always thought of as the ultimate dream job for her—buying for the entire young men's division at Nordstrom. Although stressed most of the time, she hid it well behind the perfectly blown-out hair and her designer shoes. She juggled family and a big job but still managed to have quality time for me when I needed her. Dodo was the name given to her by Samantha as a toddler when she was unable to pronounce her name, Jodi, and we all still fondly called her Dodo.

"I was celebrating being happy today," I told her, seriously having forgotten I had happiness inside myself. For the first time in years, I had woken up not wanting to kill myself. That in itself was reason to celebrate, I thought, even if it was just a random day.

But I didn't dare tell my dear friend that.

27

WHY SUICIDE?

My two childhood best friends had both lost their little brothers to suicide. One of them also lost her husband. I can still hear the call from my friend's mom. My friend's husband had never come home. He had shot himself the night before, and my friend needed me. Could I please come to Utah and help? He had left her with four small children to raise alone.

The other suicide—My friend Rachel had called me while I was walking on the beach to say her youngest brother had killed himself. "What day was it?" I asked then.

November 11 was her answer.

I shared with her what I had come to discover about that day, the 11/11 window, something I had studied since that first time I saw the shaman in Alaska. The 1111 in many spiritual traditions was a spiritual awakening code, a portal opening to the other side. This, in my opinion, was one of the only days to pass through the parallel worlds without the repercussions that would normally come when taking your own life. I knew this somewhere deep in my soul, and hopefully sharing this information gave her some comfort regarding her brother.

Suicide was not looked upon favorably within the Mormon Church, which her family was still very involved in.

Why is the world not one of acceptance and grace? One of unconditional love? Why had these people turned to suicide? I already knew the answer, for I had felt the pull of suicide too. The pull to not be on this planet. Sometimes I just didn't really want to do it anymore. The day-to-day life filled with fear, pain, and suffering—it was sometimes too much.

I'd had it all planned out in my mind. Seattle was only five hours or so from Coeur d'Alene—to the river house—to the place I planned to carry out the deed. I thought I'd give myself back to my biological father, who had carelessly helped bring me into the world. He could carelessly toss me out. After the last time we'd spoken, he had sent me a check for $3,000 and told me to never contact him again. I had asked him to help me pay for the $14,000 bill I had incurred while at the loony bin, but he hadn't cared. He had thought he could just write me off with a check for three grand.

Fuck him, I thought, let him deal with me now.

Suicide is something that is usually planned or thought out. It's not personal to family or friends who are left behind, and if I tried to explain it or talk about it, someone would certainly come knocking at my door to lock me up. Trust me, I know, it's not always easy living in a society filled to the brim with judgment, monotony, and guilt. Sensitive souls can feel this energy on every level, whether they participate in the energetic frequency or not.

I am in no way condoning or promoting suicide, but I can certainly say I understand it.

The heartache I had endured during the past years shattered me, broke me, and tore me into a million pieces and tossed me to the wind. My life was almost unbearable. I felt barely alive anyway, so what would be the difference?

The recent outpouring of suicides I had heard about was more than I could take. I had recently lost two more friends: Heather and Catherine.

The fine line between killing yourself and going to the loon is quite bleak. It often feels as if there is no other place to go for healing, at least not here, not in this country. You can do just about anything but heal yourself from the pain and internal monster of depression that sneaks up and takes so many. Nope, there's no true healing for that, not that I know of. I had certainly tried.

Back in 2016, killing myself was not out of the question. Sometimes I just didn't want to do "this." Do this bullshit, walking around pretending everything was okay when really it wasn't. Life sometimes felt like a cruel joke. I felt this way in L.A. and in Seattle, too, where countless people really are homeless, living on the streets and sleeping outside, hungry and alone. Who cared about them? Honestly, despite all the fortune I'd had, I didn't feel much different. I felt alone and, lonely, as if nobody really cared or understood me.

What I have learned, though, is that there is no place to go. The lessons only get harder, the energies thicker to transform. The answer is still the same—there really is nowhere to go, only through. The only way I knew how to get through was to be in the now—fully and completely in the now. It isn't something that comes easy or naturally. The constant mind-fucking that can often happen in the brain is something hard to contain. In yoga class it's called "monkey-mind." A mind running wild and untamed. Add some depression to the mix for any sensitive soul, and you will certainly have a recipe for unrest in our current society. Hence the reason for my wanting to leave this world—or possibly to try harder to understand it. I was on the teeter-totter ride of not wanting to belong in this life.

The holidays were here again. Once my favorite time of year when working at the beloved Nord, with its quintessential décor, it had now become my least favorite time. Staging had slowed to an almost halt, and again I wondered how I would make it financially, as well as emotionally. Nikki from Nolily had also recently lost her job. As irony would have it, we managed to get temporary jobs serving hors d'oeuvres to select clients at the fancy Nordstrom in Bellevue. We threw our pride out the window—we were no longer revered buyers for the company. We just needed to buy groceries. This time even the holiday décor seemed to have lost its luster.

I kept vowing to try my best to get through, always looking for some sort of authentic goodness. "I can do it one day at a time, one moment at a time. Living in the moment, enjoying, and finding gratitude once again in life's smallest treasures." This was my mantra, and I tried hard to practice it daily. "I am enough," I even wrote on my mirror to look at as a daily reminder to stay on the planet, to stay in the now—to stay in love and gratitude. I had given up most of my spiritual practices, but I would not give up on my internal best friend, Faith.

28

GIFT FROM THE GRAVE

I was pondering my own desire for life as I packed for my mother's celebration of life. The day she passed, I'd sent her a photo of the dishes she had given me the last time I saw her. They were perfectly displayed in the built-in glass cabinet of my 1920s apartment. I thought she would have appreciated the way I had them displayed so nicely, and the way in which they looked so perfectly at home there. The yellow of the tea set and bowls was the same yellowish color of the cabinets. The little old-school orange flowers with gold trim looked so sweet and whimsical. I was sure they had all been designed in the same era and were reunited at last.

It was the day before I left for the funeral when Savvy texted that she wanted to come. I was packing as I excitedly texted her back. "It's not too late," I typed. "You can still come." She was coming, my daughter was coming! She wanted to see me, to be there for me and to say goodbye to her grandmother. I had done something right, after all. I wasn't a terrible person, a horrible mother. I was just a very sad, broken one.

I was over the moon happy as I finished packing for my mother's funeral.

It had been three years since I'd spent any quality time with Savvy. We had met for a quick coffee a year ago while I was in San Diego seeing customers, but that was it. It was more of a check-in, as if I were an inmate or something, while her dad waited in the car outside the Starbucks. I walked her out as tears instantly sprang to my cheeks. Dave rolled down the window to ask if I was okay.

"Yes, I have just never seen her drive before," had been my response. She had left my house when she was fourteen. All the small yet monumental moments I had missed out on had broken me even more, if that was even possible.

The day after she texted me, I was so excited to see her as I waited at her gate, her flight landing in Salt Lake only half an hour after mine.

I could not believe it had been so long since I had seen my baby girl. I was a nervous wreck waiting for her flight to land. It was all I could do to hold back the tears when I finally got to see her, hug her, and breathe in her sweet smell. My stepdad and his wife picked us up from the airport, and we all drove to the small town in Cache Valley, where my mother and sister had been living for the past decade. We checked into a tiny motel and settled in. I was delighted to be having a slumber party with Savannah. I hadn't been this happy in years.

Oh, and what a funeral it was. It wasn't just a funeral, but a party, and a purple one at that. Everyone was dressed in purple—the flowers were purple, there were purple ribbons and cards—everything was absolute purple perfection. She had planned it all herself, her last chance to control it all, and she did. My mother's last ride was in a fancy, old-style Cadillac hearse. Every single detail was stunning, and she was beautiful as she finally lay at peace in her white lace gown. She had finally let go of the doubt, fear, depression, and insecurity that I felt had always plagued her. She now lay at peace. I shed no tears. Only smiles and love were on my face. Later, my sister asked if I felt there were unresolved issues with my mother and me. My immediate response was, "No, we no longer have any issues," and I meant it, saying it with such conviction that my sister never asked again.

"Where Mom is, Keri, only love exists," I said. This was my belief, and I held it to be true. The other side of life, the other side of the veil . . . known to many as heaven, hardly seemed like a place that would entertain anything other than love.

"Only love exists there," I said it again, confirming it to be so. My sister, who was always a sensitive, sweet soul and was now a Christian, could not argue the point. Or didn't want to. It didn't matter. We both chose love.

I accepted the reunion with my baby girl as an apology from my mother. I knew somehow, even from the other side of the veil, my mother had sent this precious gift. I smiled, and hugged Savvy as they lowered my mother's body into her grave. I forgave my mother, as I knew she'd given me back my baby. Now if I could only repair my relationship with Sam. I had always said she was my biggest spiritual teacher, my Angel-Face Lovey. That was my nickname for her. Savvy's nickname was Baby Girl. No matter the age, they would always be my babies.

29

ALIVE AT LAST

MAY 2017

My renewed connection with Savvy after my mom's funeral gave me the hope and drive I had really been needing—just by seeing her. Even staying with her in a crappy motel in Utah for three days was utter bliss. My dad took us to the liquor store after the funeral and bought us a bottle of champagne, which was about the only thing I could drink these days. I gladly let Savvy drink the champagne with me, even though she was only seventeen. This reunion was cause for celebration. The last few years had been more than tough; they had been heart-wrenching and indescribably painful. For both of us.

We drank champagne, laughed, danced, and told jokes with my dad and his wife until late that night after the funeral. Savvy got to see all of the many relatives she hadn't seen in a long time, and we got to do some much needed catching up. I tried to get her to tell me everything, not to leave out a detail, but it was hardly what a teen wanted to do—and it had been three years. How could I expect her to catch me up on three years in just one night? Having reconnected with Savvy, I now longed to reconnect with Sam. I tried not to talk about her too much with Savannah, but it was hard not to. Now Savvy felt the need to defend her sister and also to defend her mother, like my sister had with me and my mom. I didn't want her to have to be put in that position, and I tried not to ask about Sam. How did we heal the wounds that ran so deep, the chain of trauma repeating over and over?

Gratitude and faith, those were the only answers I knew. I did my best to stay in the present, to stay in gratitude. It was hard to see Savvy walk away again as she left the gate to get on her plane. This time she gave me a hug, said she loved me, and waved goodbye. I was content and beyond grateful, but as I walked to my own gate, the sadness of missing her again started to sink in.

Now that I had reconnected with Savvy, I missed the girls even more. I had already missed out on years of their lives. I wasn't even "allowed" to go to Samantha's high school graduation. She threatened not to go if I went. She said I would ruin her important day. Dave had called to let me know that I should respect her wishes and not come. My own daughter didn't even want me at her graduation. I had felt the slow waves of my depression creeping back since returning from my mom's funeral.

Sam's toughness had certainly served her well. Not only was she tough, but smart, beautiful, and determined. As a junior at Berkeley, and a Leukemia survivor, I doubted anything would stand in her way—certainly not her "loser mother"—her words. That was just one of the endearing terms she openly shared with me. Sam had even pledged the same sorority chapter as I had, not remembering that I, too, was an Alpha Phi. She probably wouldn't have joined had she known, but I felt comforted that she was there, getting an amazing education—an experience some kids only dreamt about. Berkeley, any college really, was a dream I had hoped would come true for her. I hadn't even seen her in college or seen Savannah go to high school, not even one day of any of it.

I had missed those crucial experiences—and many others. I didn't get to move Sam into her dorm at college, helping her settle in and decorate, or see the place where she would go to school. No matching sweatshirts, no Berkeley Mom license plate holder, no visit to her sorority, nothing. Not even one photo from her entire college experience. I often stalked the Alpha Phi Facebook page just to see her.

Maybe I hadn't been deep in a depression. Maybe I was just mourning, not even mourning the recent death of my own mother but mourning those moments that all mothers cherish.

I recently tried to explain this to a friend without children. "It's not always the big things that are the important part of being a mother. It's the day-to-day small moments." Like watching Samantha's face light up when she was excited to see me after school or tell me something new. The way her thick, white-blonde hair swept across her porcelain skin sprinkled with tiny freckles. I loved the way her twinkly, blue eyes closed when I laid my hand across her forehead, and how much she loved it. I would love nothing more than to pet her sweet head again. Or to give Savvy her lunch and a kiss while watching her ride down the steep hill of our driveway on her skateboard. I can still see her round cheeks; long, honey-caramel hair, skinny jeans, and Converses, always. I loved both girls, obviously. Sam had always been a daddy's girl, and Savvy had been my little sidekick, and I missed that. I missed our family.

My mom had been gone for two months, and I still waited to see if I would be sad or not. I hadn't cried yet, but I guessed I'd gotten that out of my system when I'd seen her last. Besides, I was too happy reconnecting with Savvy to even consider being sad while at Mom's funeral. I could still hear her, barely gone, saying, "When you grow up, I hope you have girls who are just like you, and they break your heart." Well, she had certainly gotten her wish; my heart had been broken.

But now I had at least one of them back. I had never dreamed my connection with Savvy could be broken. We'd had such a tight bond. She was sensitive and sweet yet creative and outgoing. She could light up any room with her infectious smile and the silly demeanor that kept everyone laughing. When she was a child, if I barely raised my voice around her, she would cry. I knew how she felt just by the look on her face. I missed her so much. Without her in my life, I felt a part of my own self missing—I was lost without her.

It was Mother's Day once again. This year I thought I would get a call, at least from Savvy. She had invited me down to help her get ready for her prom. I was so happy to go and see my little pretty. I missed them both so much it hurt—the grief of a mother missing her child was unlike anything I had ever experienced. It was hard not to worry about what they were doing and who they were with. Were they safe? Were they happy? As always, I tried to keep myself busy, trying to forget about the day.

Just before I went to bed, I got a text from Savvy, saying, "Happy Mother's Day."

I would take it.

I flew down in June for Savvy's prom. I couldn't wait to spend time with her and participate in her life. She looked gorgeous in her cobalt blue dress with sheer cut-outs around the neck and at the bottom. The sheer netting made it look like pretty cobalt flowers were covering all of her curvy parts. It was sexy yet sweet and feminine, just like her. Her hair was now platinum blonde, and she still had the perfect heart-shaped face and darling round cheeks. She smiled at her date, who wore a dark black suit and cobalt blue bow tie, which perfectly matched her dress. They were having a pre-party at her friend Bella's house overlooking Swami's Beach. I was so happy running around, snapping pictures of them. It was a beautiful, sunny day, and all the kids looked so sophisticated and awkwardly excited. The last time I had seen these radiant young people, they were only children. Now they struck me as being so grown-up, all dressed up with the glow of the sunset and the ocean behind them—making for a picture-perfect, magical moment.

Savvy was silly, still making funny faces and making everyone laugh, even in her grown-up gown and princess braids. I loved this girl so much. She'd always been the life of the party, ever since she was little. I was so proud to see her shine her inner light so brightly. It was all I could do not to smother her. I wanted to soak up all of her sweet beauty and goodness as if she were the setting sun herself.

30

BACK TO CALI

SUMMER 2017

It seems people from Cali get a bad name, and one thing is for sure, those who call it "Cali" are probably not from California—but to me it felt most like home. Was it because I had birthed and raised my babies there? Was it the coastal beauty that attracted me—the endless sunsets that never grew old? The skies often started in a pink and purple cotton candy blend of beauty. Sometimes the clouds seemed to dance through the sunset sky, leaving behind a palette of purple, pink, orange, and blue perfection.

I had been dreaming of going back home since the second I boarded the plane back to Seattle. After this last visit with Savvy, I had been longing to go back. But how could I make it work? I sat on the floor of my Seattle apartment on a big, orange silk rug, my mind in wonder at the sunsets in California, and just like that, the answer came. I would share whatever I could to get back to my children, including my darling apartment.

I jumped up and excitedly cleaned, fluffed, and perfected every detail of my tiny Seattle apartment. I snapped pictures of its cute details and shared its amazing location, nestled just blocks away from the Space Needle, and excitedly loaded them onto Airbnb. I had spent the past three years perfecting places just like this—designing spaces and making them darling. I went to bed dreaming of California and woke up to five bookings. I was going home, and I wasn't sure when I would be back to Seattle.

I called my friend Marci and rented a room in Encinitas for a couple months. I bought new sheets and towels for my soon-to-be guests and once again packed up my little car for the long drive down the coast. These bookings, although illegal in my building, would fund my way. My super-nice neighbor (of course, also named Nicole) agreed to buzz my guests into our 1920s apartment building.

I had made up my mind. I was going to spend the summer at home, walking the beach and hanging out with Savvy. I was so excited—thrilled about my decision.

Savvy, of course, was lovely and helped me settle in and decorate my new room. It was temporary, and I hoped to see her as much as possible. We picked up burritos and hung out. She now wanted her tarot cards read.

She had always been a magical child who was extremely lucky when she put her mind to something. She'd been the grand prize winner at a school event the first year the iPad came out. It was at the sock-hop, a fifties-inspired fundraiser at the school, and I just happened to be the PTA mom in charge of the event. I was selling raffle tickets at the entrance to the dance when Savvy came up to the table with the twenty-dollar bill I had given her, along with a mischievous smile. "Oh no, you can't win, someone will think I cheated," I told my then seven-year-old.

"Oh yeah, Mama, I am gonna win," she had said. Neither of us had been very surprised when the DJ host pulled Savvy's number from the spinning vat.

She lived in the moment and was always full of fun and vitality. She was savvy like that, yes, she was, and I was so pleased to be back in her presence. I read her cards for her in my beach apartment and kissed her on the head as she left, feeling blessed to be with her.

A few weeks after I'd arrived in Encinitas, my friends and I walked the few blocks from Angi's to another friend's house by the Del Mar beach for the usual Fourth of July regatta. Our crew had been doing this tradition in Del Mar for twenty years, maybe more. Everyone paraded out to the beach together, carrying blow-up "yachts" while singing the national anthem and taking whatever drinks we could carry. Once out past the breakers, we all tied together and spent the day in the sun drinking and laughing. We were offshore, so drinks were allowed, due to some maritime law, or maybe one that had been made up; I wasn't sure. Most of my friends were now pushing fifty, but that didn't slow this crew down—they were always fun and entertaining.

That's when I broke my toe. Or, at least, I thought I did. I told my friend, who thought I was overreacting. The day was just getting started, and I was even sober when I rolled my foot on the uneven sidewalk at our friend's place.

"Come on, lets jump on the big paddle board—I am part owner," my friend justified once we were in the water. We jumped onto the ten-man stand-up board. It took four guys to paddle out past the big surf, and we parade-waved on the way out, laughing at our genius. I was in a lot of pain, but still didn't cry as I knew I was in good company; two friends were doctors and one a nurse. What else could I do? I thought. I might as well stay and soak my toe in the ocean while drinking with my friends. All was fine until I had to get out of the water and walk. Luckily it was only a small hop back to Jake's house, where I hurried to put my foot in the beer cooler. My doctor friend came around the corner.

"Ut-oh," she said. "That doesn't look so good."

"Yeah, I think I broke my toe," I replied.

She took a quick look then said, "Nope, but you did break your foot!"

Then they came, the tears. Not from the pain—it didn't hurt that bad. But I had just landed a new job where I was supposed to start working the next day as a designer for a large bohemian-eclectic furniture store. How was I going to walk around the floor of the big store? Luckily, I was staying with my doctor friend for the next few days. Before the end of the day, my crew had rounded up a boot for my broken foot and a scooter to ride around in the store.

This injury—which would take a while to heal—also meant that I wouldn't be able to return to my three-story walk-up in Seattle in three months as I'd planned. Another forced change, I supposed. This change, though unplanned, I was secretly happy about.

I thanked the universe.

My super nice designer friends in Seattle packed up my tiny apartment for me. I had already depersonalized the place, packing up most of my cherished items, knowing I'd be gone for the summer. I was sad to not say goodbye to my friends, or to my place, but happy to not have to run into the sweet man who owned the building. He and I had spent countless hours talking about architecture, furniture, and the history of Seattle. He was now quite upset with me for subletting my place and was glad to see me go. I had always prided myself in being a good girl, for doing the right thing. These days though, I was definitely more of a rule breaker.

I showed up for my first day of work at Caravan West with a broken foot and a scooter. It was a big corner store downtown in my small coastal community. Luckily, the place was several thousand square feet, and I could fly around the store on my scooter. I loved merchandising, of course, and the broken foot didn't slow me down. In fact, I could scoot around much faster than I could have walked the large concrete floor. The day I started, the owner asked if I could also be the manager of the place. She hadn't realized I had an extensive retail background when she hired me, and now she wanted a little more bang for her buck. Or so I suspected.

I kindly declined.

I hadn't managed my own store—why would I want to manage hers? I didn't do schedules, payroll, order entry, and inventory management. I didn't like to do any of those tasks. I told her I'd happily hang all the giant pieces of art, move all the furniture, and remerchandise all the overpriced clothing, bikinis, and jewelry. I'd be happy to do all of this while selling my ass off and ensuring every detail in the store was perfect and that every customer was greeted and sold to. And yes, this I could do all on one fucking foot. But manage the store I would not do.

But this boss didn't like my answer and didn't really like me. I wasn't terribly fond of her either. She talked shit about every cute girl who she hired, then fired them for not doing anything but be cute, even though that's exactly why she hired them. I stood up for them—I called her out, and she didn't like it.

After three months, I could finally walk. It was one of the first mornings I walked into work at Caravan West, and Roberto was waiting for me. Roberto and I had stayed friends ever since we met that day at Home Depot, and he had painted the inside of my house before my divorce. He had worked for many of my friends since then and was here to do a favor for me. I had asked if he could install a remote control for the fancy light fixture that was impossible to turn on without using a tall ladder to reach. It was such a safety hazard, and easily remedied. Besides, there was no way I was going to climb that tall ladder myself with my foot still fragile from the break. So, I had asked Roberto to come in and set up a remote.

Another employee, the right-hand woman of the owner, was there and called me into the office.

I said, "Sure, as soon as Roberto finishes with the remote."

Eager to be in control, she weirdly said Roberto would have to come back another time, that she needed to speak with me right away.

I said goodbye to Roberto and walked into the back office as she introduced me to the new store manager. It was her first day, and she was there to fire me. I wasn't surprised that the coward of a store owner hadn't even shown up to do it herself. Apparently, they couldn't afford a store manager and an in-house designer. This girl would be taking over my merchandising duties as well as managing the store.

"Fine," I said, not even flinching, "I will wait for my paycheck."

"You know we can't write you a check, Kami," said the owner's friend.

"That's okay," I said. "I will just sit and wait. You do know that at the time of termination in the state of California, it is required by law that you have an employee's check ready when you fire them."

She clearly didn't know the law in California, or she would have written me a check. They were not that smart; they should have at least waited to have the free remote installed, but instead she had rudely dismissed Roberto. I was pissed as I tried to storm out of the giant store on my still-tender broken foot, but it was more like a hobble.

Hadn't I written this "hired and fired" chapter already—the one of everyday dumbasses, myself included? I was angry and tired of bending to society. I didn't fit into their norm. Now what did I do with my not-so-normal self and the twenty-four dollars I had to my name?

31

GAMBLING MY $800

I f you are going to gamble with life, you may as well go all in! That was my thought process, anyway.

I went home without my stupid paycheck. I was still mad at myself for getting fired, wondering why I had taken the stupid job in the first place. I had just kind of fallen into it, caught up in the beauty of the big store and its contents, wanting to play in there and design the place, move around all the pretty furniture. Now what? I looked up my unemployment benefits. I certainly wouldn't get far on the $167 a week that the state of California would offer. Not that I could really live on the twenty-five-dollars-an-hour I was currently making, not here, and not in Seattle. I had somehow managed to live off that hourly rate for years now, but it was more like existing, and I was far from thriving. At the moment, I had less than thirty dollars to my name. But I did have almost a full tank of gas, so that was a plus.

A week later I got my last paycheck, all $800 dollars of it. I cashed it and off to L.A. I went. If I spent the money towards rent or food, I would have nothing, I reasoned. I mindfully chose items that were sure to sell to a handful of loyal Luv thing customers. I still had my amazing customers.

178

All I had was me, and my It's a luv thing brand name.

"I've got this!" I said to myself, trying on my confidence as I drove to L.A. to the Fashion District to invest my $800. I planned to revive my Luv thing business.

I had trust in myself. I had nothing to fear. I was a badass motherfucker, I kept reminding myself. I had zero interest in contributing to the slave society role that the world deemed as a j-o-b.

And the jobs hadn't wanted me.

Again and again, I had to trust in myself. I kept my head down and focused on my work and my relationship with Savvy. That year I somehow turned $800 into 26K in sales, and 65K in sales the next. I paid my rent late more times than not, reinvesting my money in product instead. I went to L.A. weekly, sometimes with only a few hundred dollars to spend. I always came home with no money for food, and always running on fumes of gas. It was almost a game, one that I was determined to play well. Running multimillion-dollar businesses was fun, stressful, and rewarding, but this last investment in myself really made me proud. I had come a long way, but I was still barely surviving—or eating, for that matter. I was used to bare cupboards though—they had been that way for years now.

I decided to move to Palm Springs. Since I could not afford to live in Encinitas, and I wasn't working every day, I reasoned it was a good move. I wanted to root in and try to write. I needed to transform my years of journaling and pain, lay them out and let them go, always looking for the higher purpose in the lesson.

I had always wanted to live in Palm Springs, so here was my chance. I really hated where I lived in the burbs of Carlsbad, the next town over from Encinitas and the only place I could find to live when I moved back from Seattle. The last flood of rain had come in sideways from the wall heater into my tiny studio apartment, soaking my silk rug. That had been the last straw.

When I found the place in Palm Springs, it was newly renovated, and the landlord offered a month of free rent. I was so excited to be the first to move in. The pool was right outside my front door, and there was a pickleball court. I loved the private back patio where I planted flowers and succulents. It was also across the street from the Ace Hotel, where my friends' band played once a month, but I was still very lonely. It was summer and hot in Palm Springs. The place certainly wasn't filling up very fast. There was one new tenant, then there were three, and then a couple more. It was not going to be the glamourous "Palm Springs life" I had envisioned—no cute, white tennis skirts to wear while playing pickleball. There were no foxy boys by the pool, fluffing my martini, not that I could really drink much these days. Alcohol and I had a slow and tumultuous break up over the years. One by one, no more wine, vodka, or beer—they all went away. My body could no longer tolerate any of them, but I wasn't too keen to give them up. Alcohol has often been deemed as low vibration. No wonder it is called "spirits." And they aren't the good kind.

Palm Springs was lovely, but not what I had expected. The darling mid-century building with a pool wasn't the paradise I had wished for. I had almost cooked myself to death when the AC was broken and I didn't realize it. I was so sick with severe dehydration in the 120-degree heat that I could hardly move. Luckily, I had one friend, Holli, who lived close by and came over to save me with fluids and food. She helped me move a couple things to the apartment next door while they fixed the air conditioner. Holli had a super sweet demeanor and was a true friend—the only one I really had in the desert. I did make friends with two neighbors. One was a gay male prostitute, and the other a girl from L.A. who had also been in the clothing business. But I didn't really fit in with either of them. Or anyone for that matter.

The year had flown by, and my one-year lease was already up. I felt I had not accomplished anything other than getting another layer of wrinkles. The building had recently been sold, soon to become a boutique hotel. I was out of time to live in this funky mid-century modern apartment.

Even though I couldn't afford it, I missed my little beach town, my community, and a few friends. I didn't see Savvy as much as I would have liked. She was busy and in high school, but we talked often, and I was happy when we were able to be together. I wanted to participate in her life more, and living in Palm Springs wasn't that easy. My business was slowly gaining traction as I continued to invest as much as I could, increasing my inventory and reconnecting with customers. It was time to somehow move back to the coast. Even the bright sunshine of Palm Springs could not shed enough light to ease my deep, dark fear of the future.

32

MOONLIGHT

May 2019

I had finally gotten myself up and motivated, and I started taking walks again on a great, little loop close to my apartment in Palm Springs. I enjoyed wandering through my eclectic neighborhood, then down to the Tahquitz Riverbed. This loop was spectacular that afternoon. I saw cute little jackrabbits, squirrels, and birds of all sorts. The desert was so serene and mysterious. I often got up super early just to see the sun rise on the mountains, displaying them in an ethereal pink glow that was always so magnificent. The sky had the same kind of glow that afternoon when I left my apartment. It was dusk and the full moon was about to come up. As I walked around the bend to the riverbed, an incredible, bright yellow moon popped up in the pink sky and sat among the tall palm trees. The moon was so clear and big and bold it felt like you could almost reach out and pluck it from the sky. The beauty was so magical that I just sat myself down, right there on the dirt trail, to say thanks.

"Thank you, moon, for reflecting back such beauty, thank you for making me feel like you are listening, thank you for watching, for knowing my every move. Show me that my life and existence have meaning, oh sweet moon—what will I do now? Where will I live? Please guide me with your beauty and grace."

I prayed with my heart so open that I was sure the moon had heard me, as I complemented her picturesque beauty and asked for her light to shine on me.

A few days later, while in Leucadia seeing a customer, my phone rang. It was an unknown number, but I answered because it could have been a customer. It wasn't.

"Hi there, I got your number from a tenant of mine. I am not sure you even know her, but she said she is a friend of a friend of yours. Anyway, we have an opening in our apartment building here in Leucadia, which we never have, and the girl who was planning to move in now can not. Are you still interested?"

"Yes, yes, I am!" I said excitedly.

"I know you live in Palm Springs, so I'm not sure when you would be able to see it, and I would really like to rent it by the end of the month, which is less than ten days away," said the landlady.

"I am in town now," I said. "I can be there in ten minutes! And yes, yes, I can definitely move in by the end of the month!"

Driving over, I was beyond elated. The apartment building was on the west side of Highway 101, just two blocks from Moonlight Beach, and probably had the cheapest rent in all of Encinitas.

"I'll take it," I said to the manager as soon as I saw it—a small, funky 1950s apartment building. There were fourteen units surrounding a giant jacaranda tree, rose garden, orange trees, and a great little spot of dirt in front of the available apartment where I could garden. I could hardly believe my luck. It was just blocks from downtown and the beach. They only rented to friends and family and never advertised, which was probably why the rent was so affordable. I filled out the application, somehow overlooking the credit check part, and excitedly handed it over to the manager. He didn't ask and never did run the credit check. The apartment was mine if I wanted it.

As I drove back to Palm Springs, I said a silent word of thanks to the full moon as I smiled up again in appreciation of her blessings and beauty.

Next, I just had to miraculously come up with three grand in less than a week! Somehow, I always managed. This time, I even asked my ex for money. Pride was a thing of the past. He even helped me move a couple of things and gave me $500 towards the deposit.

I didn't feel bad or obligated to pay him back because he had never bothered to pay the judge-ordered $600-a-month alimony. I really could have used the money over the years, but he had been taking sole care of our children. I'd had to move on, forwards, not backwards.

We had somehow mended. I had forgiven him—he had been a good father, and finally, somewhere along the way, we'd found peace. Maybe the prayers I had been saying were once again working. I had been doing the Hawaiian prayer when thinking of him for years now. I had learned the Ho'oponopono when I met the beautiful people of Molokai, and since Dave felt so connected to the islands, I had decided to use this prayer for our healing. The meaning of the prayer is, "I'm sorry. Please forgive me. Thank you, I love you." The Hawaiian people often sat in a circle surrounding those who had a dispute, and until the dispute between the people was settled, the community waited and supported them. The Hawaiians knew the energetic dis-ease would cause disease within their community. Once again, I felt our communities lacked the tools to help create the best for all. This prayer was to put things back into balance, to make things right.

I would always love Dave. When he was helping me move a few things into the apartment, somewhere among the boxes of crap, I asked for his forgiveness and thanked him for taking such good care of our children. He responded with a smile and a short hug. I welcomed this new sense of balance. I met my lovely next-door neighbors, Tim and his wife—she, of course, was another Nicole. I knew I was in the right place.

I quickly settled into my new place, trying to reunite with customers and friends as well as make plans with Savannah. She and I met for lunch or dinner and to get our nails done. Or she would just stop by for a hello, which I loved and looked forward to. Connecting with customers was easy—friends not so much. I had always had such an easy time with friends, but now I didn't have the tolerance for everyday small talk. I wanted so badly to connect, to laugh and have fun, but I found that I just wasn't the same person anymore. I was still too badly broken to be fun. Society felt like a stranger. Sadly, fear and loneliness had become my new norm.

33

THE MASTURBATION
INFORMATION

July 25, 2019

I had just moved in, and I started working more, seeing customers more, and seeing Savvy more. I was grateful to be back in the swing of life and settling into my cute little coastal apartment. I was feeling better about life than I had in a while, but I was still very single. After all the masturbation talk, I had enjoyed getting to know my body.

Although one of my first attempts at masturbation just happened to have been in public in front of my once friend, I finally learned to master the deed. Through many inward mental gymnastics, as well as quite a few trips to the sex shop, I now owned an impressive toy box and knew how my body worked. There would be no depending on men for those needs. Once again, I had to be in control of my life as much as possible. I never suspected, however, that the once not-so-funny story of masturbation at SRF might also be one that led to my healing on a physical level. I knew my body well and knew something was not quite right. I felt as though I had a cyst or tumor, so I made an appointment to see my gynecologist. After the pelvic exam, she said I was fine. I told her I wasn't. I had already scheduled an ultrasound with her, so she said she would take a look. She was quite surprised to see the large, black blob on the screen and did not anticipate good news.

Although she was a surgeon herself, she referred me to a gynecologic oncologist. The tumor would have to be removed, and it could not be biopsied, for fear of it spreading. A few weeks later I went in for surgery. Savvy was waiting in my room when I woke up from the anesthesia, and she wasn't too happy with me as she looked around.

"Mom! Why didn't you tell me you were going to the cancer center! You didn't tell me they thought your tumor was cancerous," she said sternly. Savvy was a bit mad at me. She was also concerned, as her best friend's mom was on the same floor, just down the hall, battling serious ovarian cancer.

"Oh, Savannah, I slowly slurred, "everything is protons, neutrons, and electrons." I watched as she rolled her eyes at me, and I continued. "If I would have told you, or told others, they would have been worried, and their energy could be stronger than my own, because fear is strong like that. Then when the surgeon goes in to do the surgery, her observation as well as energies from others could decide my outcome. This way, I got to decide. The energy was pure, it was only mine, and the doctor was the observer."

It's just science.

I had already decided that the worst-case scenario would be a full hysterectomy and no follow-up chemo. Going in, I knew I had a tumor to be removed, along with probably my ovaries and tubes as well. The doctor came in and told Savvy and I just that.

She went on to say, "We have never seen such a tumor and we have sent it off to Harvard for further study. Your tumor was malignant; However, it was encased in a benign fluid, keeping it from spreading."

Still drugged, I casually commented, "Oh yeah, I changed my mind recently and decided to live." I was serious, I knew how powerful the mind and body could be. She looked at me as though I was crazy. But I was used to that by now, and I didn't care that the doctor didn't take me seriously.

Besides, I had a very smart tumor. It was going to Harvard!

34

BACK ON THE SACRED SAUCE

It had been years since I had done most of my spiritual practices. Daily meditations, yoga, and endless hours of research and reading were things of the past. I'd never believed in television (telling lies to your vision). I'd always felt people spent hours and hours dumping garbage into their brains, being brainwashed and programmed by the devices (duh-vice) they willingly paid for without even realizing the addiction the vices caused.

I had come full circle, moving back to the same beach community in Encinitas, just blocks from where I had raised my children. I had moved all over this town and all the way to Seattle to escape myself and my pain. And now here I was, back where I had started. Could this be the little place I'd been searching for that day back in 2007 when I left through my front gate? I felt like I'd had to come back here to pick up the pieces and reclaim myself. The hours I spent in the garden with my beloved succulents helped to ground me. I loved how easily you could break them off and put them back in the ground, "properly propagating" them. I would tell them how sorry I was for their pain as I broke them off to form new little groupings, new families, and new friends.

I loved the plants and connected with them as I moved them around in my garden. I felt as though they really called to me. Gardening was what I loved doing most. It connected me to the earth and put me in that natural meditative state that gave me such inner peace. I loved seeing the plants grow and flourish.

By now, I had actual friends calling. Jen had magically walked through the doors of It's a luv thing when I'd needed to hire someone. I had asked for someone to help me at work, to be my assistant and get me organized. A couple of hours later, she'd knocked on the window before we were quite open. She had been looking for a job, and I hired her on the spot. She set her handbag down and started right then—that was fifteen years ago. Now she was calling to see if I wanted to go to a slumber party. Speaking of plants, she explained that it would be a plant-medicine kind of party. She was planning a weekend retreat in Idyllwild, and there would be sound healing and breathwork, intention setting, journaling, meditation, and new connections with like-minded people. I decided to go—to open myself up, look at my pain, share it, and hopefully release it. What did I have to lose? I felt as though I had lost everything already, besides the broken version of myself, and I longed to put myself back together.

The house in Idyllwild was charming. Hand-carved wood made up the staircase and much of the wraparound deck. It had a big loft with many beds for all the new lady friends. There were twelve of us for the three-day weekend. There was also a guest house full of handsome Native American art as well as an old-style loom and a basket full of yarns and tapestries. This was the space where we gathered in circle to set our intentions for the weekend. I felt right at home in the place, even though I only knew a few of the women. They were all very kind, and most were somewhat new to their spiritual journey. I loved and respected their open hearts and trusted them to hold the space for my own personal inner journey.

After the first night of taking magic mushrooms and not getting much sleep, I was full of pent-up anxiety and decided to try a little "vine of the soul," or DMT—Dimethyltryptamine—a plant medicine used in many spiritual ceremonies, mostly in South America. It is often called the spirit molecule. DMT is a quick trip, with ten to twenty minutes of sometimes scary, yet very eye-opening experiences that take you right to your core, dark or light. This medicine is in the same family as Ayahuasca, but taking it is not an all-nighter, not as serious. Aya, I called her—the woman who sat at the core of the earth, the big mama, the deep vine of Gaia—Mother Earth.

As we were getting ready, I remembered the last Ayahuasca ceremony that I had felt called to participate in. It had been in the Hollywood Hills.

I say "called," because that is exactly what it is, a calling. If you are meant to meet the Great Mother Spirit who is alive and powerful, then you will be called. Preparing yourself to meet her, however, is not always an easy task, and you may not meet her on your first try. Only those who are ready will have the honor. Cleansing and fasting for a few weeks before is always a prerequisite. Then, while in the ceremony, you must also purge yourself of impurities before you will be graced by her overwhelming presence. This purging comes after drinking tea made from two plants, magically made together, which are found mostly in Peru, Ayahuasca's place of origin. This lovely purging comes in the form of vomiting and shitting out some pretty gnarly stuff that often looks and seems not of this world. The Ayahuasca ceremony is certainly not for the faint of heart—you have to be ready—ready to look at your life with all its complexities; breaking it down, letting it go, and seeing the light and splendor in everything. You see the absolute perfection, that even things that come in the form of obstacles are also perfection, but most of all, you see your own unlimited potential.

This last ceremony had been in a small, modest house all the way up a narrow, winding road at the top of the Hollywood Hills. I hadn't known anyone there other than the shaman I had been working with over the past year. All dressed in white, like everyone else, I'd quietly snuggled in with my blankets and pillows for the long night of meditation and ceremony. I remember looking at my life that night as a picture book filled with pages of ugly shit. And then it came: it crept in and enveloped my entire body, crippling me with fear. I kept trying to calm myself. This was not my first ceremony. I kept telling myself, "You are okay. Breathe through this, accept the healing, be open." I tried hard to relax, finding comfort in the sound of the continuous prayers being chanted by the shaman.

It was as if I was going down a dark tunnel, one of horror, sadness, and extreme fear. I just kept going, spiraling out of control—I had no other choice. I couldn't stop what was happening; I couldn't stop the beams of color that were streaming through my body or the weird energies I felt coming off myself. It was foreign and strange and scary. My body started to shake uncontrollably as I silently cried for myself. This state seemed to last forever, though I am sure it didn't. All of a sudden, the tunnel ended, and as it did, my soul broke out into a million bright, shining pieces—fragmented, yet all-encompassing. It felt as though somehow I'd just become a star, whatever that meant—words were incapable of expressing the meaning of what had just happened to me. What did this mean, to become a star?

Of course, this was all just theoretical, I suspected. But I knew it was more "real" than my day-to-day life. I had broken out of the chains, from the layers that had held me back and the limited thinking that tells us what we can and cannot do. I didn't know it at the time, but this would be my last all-night meditation ceremony. The other attendees were there from all over the world, and although it was a small ceremony, we knew we were called. We were all very quiet and serious. We felt it was our job to help clear the energies in this beautiful, palatial place called earth. But why there, why L.A.? I wasn't sure, but I felt as though something dark was happening beneath the surface in this city. I didn't question why; I just came when called. We all intuitively knew ahead of time this circle would be gathering.

The shaman, who sang his magical Icaros, the healing prayers that he chanted throughout the night, shared his experience first as the morning sun crept into the quiet and serene house. Like steadfast warriors, we had spent the night holding the line of the spiritual warfare that continued to rage through the world. Like the night, this warfare felt dark, usually unseen by normal society but felt and known about by some, nonetheless. This darkness had crept into every aspect of our lives, and we had unconsciously submitted. We were doing our best to help overcome this unknown shadow, to break up these dark energies and help to raise the vibration of the planet. To make room for love and light.

"I saw Kami turn into a star," the shaman joyfully blurted out. "It was amazing; she just burst into a million tiny pieces, transforming."

I was overwhelmed and nodded as tears of joy slid down my cheeks. How could he know that I'd had this experience, that I'd felt this unknown magic, this energy field, or other dimension?

My own immediate answer was, "Just because it isn't taught in Western culture or talked about doesn't mean it isn't real." I sat in my knowing, sure that everything would eventually be okay.

I had sat there in the Hollywood Hills, knowing that I had just become a star. Though it was hardly the Hollywood Star most dreamed of becoming. I'd take it.

At the retreat in Idyllwild, remembering the Hollywood Hills experience, I now eased back onto the pillows and slowly closed my eyes, surrounded by beautiful, loving women who held space for my expansion. I waited to connect with the medicine that had become part of me, and I anxiously waited for the answers to all my many questions.

"An egg?" I laughed out loud as I saw the egg and all the many limbs she had, each arm coming closer and closer. I tried to see what was in each hand. I found this quite hilarious, as eggs usually were not a certain gender. Nor do they have arms or legs. Its patterns, dimensions, and colors were not of this world, but I knew it was somehow real—probably just beyond what we were capable of seeing, because we wouldn't believe it if we did.

This egg had multiple arms and legs—each dancing delightfully as if it were Shiva herself. Each limb held a beautiful card. As the arms came towards me, I realized we all had choices—we were all dealt cards. We chose them; we had already picked. We chose the path on which we wanted to go, the lessons we wanted to learn, the life and person we wanted to grow into to give us the experiences we deemed necessary to grow.

At least I knew then, the egg definitely came before the chicken! My mother popped into my mind, and her chicken.

Growing up, Mom always collected chickens. Not live ones, just decorative ones. Then she said she didn't like people who were chicken shits, so she decided to start collecting roosters. She said we should all be the cock of our own walk.

My mother, she was classic.

The last present she sent me was a fucking chicken.

"What do I want a metal chicken for," I asked her over the phone.

"When I die, you will have it to remind you of me."

"I needed a chicken for that?" I laughed.

But the chicken now resided in my garden. I moved her often to give her a better view, a different perspective, to remind me not to be a chicken shit as I left my apartment each day.

And just like that, during my DMT journey, the chicken-egg gave me the card I had wanted.

Just then, I heard an echo of my mother's voice.

"Get yourself together, don't be a chicken shit! It's time to be the cock of your own walk!"

Thanks, Mom, I thought. You really do love me, don't you? I laughed out loud.

Fear cripples us, enslaves us, and takes away our lives.

I finally cared that I had been missing out on life. My vow to stay asleep had worked, but it wasn't the answer. Presence and healing were the answers.

Becoming my highest and best self was the answer, even if it scared the shit out of me. I knew we were all aspects of God; it was something I had learned over and over again during my many years of studying spiritual texts and prophecies. Everyone was an aspect of God—I wasn't special. But I was special because I was an aspect of God reflecting my God-self in this current life as Kami. We were all creating our own world, and reflecting it, as OUR-Selves.

The rest of the retreat was fun and rejuvenating, sitting by the pond watching the fish, going on walks, and sitting at the picnic table with the ladies and watching the stars. It was refreshing to meet new women, coming together from all over San Diego to support one another on our healing journies.

We stepped out of the fear that had swept the world, even if it was only for the weekend.

35

IS IT WRITTEN IN THE STARS?

After the weekend ceremony in Idyllwild, I decided to treat myself to a new astrology reading for my birthday. I was calling upon the stars for direction. It had been twelve years since the last one, which had put me into a tailspin. My astrologer friend Kimberly had come over then to my place to give me a reading. The 2008 recession and my looming divorce had been kicking my ass, and I'd needed some direction.

"You should write a book," she had said. "Writing is all over your astrology."

I had been writing as a means of healing, purging my emotions onto the page or into my computer for decades. My rage and hate had filled pages and pages, but I'd had no plans of sharing any of it. I just had to get it out of my body and put it somewhere safe, not unlike the time I'd left a piece of my heart in the unframed closet of my childhood house. My anger was hidden now in my writing, where nobody would see or hear, and I'd had no plans to share the pain with anyone.

Kimberly and I had sat in my apartment in 2008, overlooking the impressive ocean view. I'd sat legs-crossed, as usual, on my big, round Z-Gallery chair and immediately fell over into the pillow and cried out loud after hearing that according to her, and my guides—I should write a book. I could not stop the ugly cry from pouring out of my soul then. She had really hit a chord with me. She had sat there somewhat perplexed by my response.

After I'd stopped crying and settled down, Kimberly had asked, "Why did that upset you so much?"

My response had been barely audible. "Wasn't it bad enough that I had to live through all of these experiences, all this shit? And now, you're telling me I should write a book about them, share it? One woman can only take so much," I'd told her.

And that had been before Dave had taken the girls away from me. I had been completely clueless to the depths of pain that one could endure. Being sexually abused by my father— that was tough—having a child with leukemia was definitely tough. Divorce, closing my business, all tough. Going to the mental hospital, twice, while having the whole town talk about you, and your poor children having to carry around the burden of being told they had a mentally ill mother—that was hard too. But losing my children? It absolutely crippled me; nothing could prepare me for that. It was a pain I could barely confront, let alone share. But somehow, I knew I had to, maybe even back then in 2008 when I sat down with Kimberly.

Now, in 2020, as I walked across the street to meet Elizabeth for my birthday reading, I was looking for a little extra confirmation. Because of the pandemic, I had nothing but time—it was the perfect time to write. It was time to finish it up or throw it out. I just needed some clear answers about my looming writing project. I ordered some coffee and sat down, grateful that this week small businesses could be open, and we could meet in person.

Elizabeth had been a loyal customer at my boutique—I had been selling clothing to her for years. I had heard that her astrology readings were quite good, and I looked forward to hearing what she had to say. She could hardly wait to get started either.

I had barely sat down when the first thing out of her mouth was, "Kami, you are going to think I am absolutely crazy, but have you ever considered writing a book? You're not just writing a book this next year but publishing a book! It is all over your chart, you just have to do it—have you started writing?"

She continued with her excitement as I listened.

"Also, you may get a small inheritance to help you take a break and get this book published. It won't come easy. You will have to work for it, but it should come."

"No, no inheritance," I said. "Nobody is leaving me any money, definitely not."

"Well, there is a possibility—just keep yourself open to it. I mean, it won't be large enough to live on, but it should give you the respite and funds you need to help publish your book.

I mean, have you ever even considered writing? You almost need to totally quit your job and get this book finished. I know you think I am crazy right now," she continued.

I shook my head in disbelief. "No," I finally said while laughing. "I certainly don't believe you are crazy."

Four days later, I arrived home to find a thick stack of paperwork leaning against my door. I was scared, knowing that kind of document rarely held anything good. But I was wrong. I read through the fat stack. My great-aunt Jean had passed three years prior, leaving part of her estate to my grandma, who had also passed. The estate then went to my mom and then to my siblings and me. Great-Aunt Jean's estate had been in probate for three years. For three years they had been looking for us, finally hiring a private investigator to track us down, trying to tie up the loose ends of her estate. Like the astrologer had said, it wouldn't be enough to live on, but it was enough to help develop my book and share my story.

Sharing this story had never been my plan, never something I thought I would be doing. But somewhere deep inside of myself, I did know and feel that the Spiritual Me, the real me, the one who was screaming and jumping up and down with delight in some distant past or previous realm, had my story all planned out.

I can almost hear and see myself saying, "Pick me. Pick me. I'll do it! I'll help! I want to be part of the awakening! I'll help pioneer—I can do it."

Hopefully sharing this story will help add some sparks to this prophesied awakening of the planet.

Maybe, just maybe, it really is written in the stars.

36

BEHIND THE IRON CURTAIN

It was now Christmas 2020, and the year from hell for many. Pain and fear had been served up on a giant platter, and the entire world had been invited. The playing field had been leveled—businesses closed, couples divorced, and children struggled. Suicide and death were things we heard about daily. The mass division over opinions had encouraged the ugliest of behaviors in humans we once called friends. But did anyone truly want to know the root of all the nastiness going on in the world? Did anyone want to know of the dark octopus holding all the cards, monopolizing every aspect of our lives?

It amazed me how caught up everyone was becoming in the shaming and blaming of each other over who had the best political puppet or the best medical knowledge. I had known a spiritual war was coming. The vision of this world change was one of the things I'd channeled on the first day I'd gone to the loon. Somehow, I now thought I could help. I wanted to help.

"God said, 'Wake up'" was the first thing I'd written in my very first computer long ago. That first journal entry had been written shortly after I'd had my first astrology reading,

200

which had said, "You have the key, it is hidden deep inside yourself—the key to knowing, higher learning, compassion, and love."

At the time, I had thought the term "God said 'Wake up'" was so interesting. It was not something people really talked about, waking up. Back then, I had hardly known what it meant myself. I thought it meant getting up early in the wee hours of the night, tapping into the solace and silence and then listening. The magical hours, the God hours. So that is what I'd done. I often got up early in the morning, unable to stop the information that felt as though it wanted to pour out of my soul. I'd obviously had no plans of sharing any of those writings and had never thought writing could be something I would enjoy.

Maybe, just maybe, I did have the key. I thought there was only one key to this higher knowledge, and I had always believed this key to be love. I had designed and sold many T-shirts depicting sayings of love, yet I had certainly not changed the world one T-shirt at a time like I'd once had big dreams of doing.

My philosophies—I had written down many times that "We are all particles of God; we are God."

We held the creative energy and power inside ourselves to create our own reality, if only we could be quiet enough to listen. That's what waking up meant for me.

Listening.

The only answer I knew was oneness and love. Did we honestly want to know what was keeping us from this unlimited potential?

Could we actually handle the truth? I'd never thought my spiritual path of endless studies would lead me down the rabbit hole to the root of power that controlled every aspect of society.

Back in 2007, I had most certainly sounded like a crazy person, telling the stories of worldwide monopolies.

Life really was a board game, after all, and we were playing into it.

We have been played.

Divide and conquer—that's how the elites have set it up, leaving us to battle it out amongst ourselves as they sit pretty in the great tower of goodness. They even openly admit their only purpose is to make money, that "they"—the billionaires—could care less about humanity. They only care about making money.

If we really want to know what's going on in the world, we should follow the money. There certainly has been a great shift of money since the pandemic. The billionaires effortlessly got richer as the middle class slowly moved towards extinction and small business owners struggled to keep the doors open.

We are enslaved by a small elite society of the world, and we don't even see the way we submissively consent to imprisoning ourselves.

We have been poisoned by the food and the water, then drugged by big pharma, all while giving most of our money to these people who were already billionaires. These same elites fund both sides of all wars and both political parties, for huge amounts of profit.

The ones who claim to get you well are also the ones who made you sick in the first place.

Do we believe that the government puppets who do their bidding care about us? A perfect, yet small example—is the fluoride in the water because the government cares about your teeth? No, they don't care about your teeth; they care about keeping you asleep, manipulating you to believe what they want you to believe. They tell you one thing is good, all while poisoning us, putting fluoride in the water, not only for slow poisoning but to calcify the pineal gland, the gland to higher learning. The pineal gland is the gateway to higher knowing, to our higher self. Our God Self. If only we could wake up to this knowing; if only there were an alarm clock for waking up society.

Follow the money to see who sits behind the iron curtain. It goes so far back, and like everything else in the world, it is all mindfully mapped out. When you follow the money, you will find out who "they" really are. The old-world banking money goes so far back and is intentionally hidden and intertwined in worldwide politics, religion, and Corporatocracy. It owns and operates all aspects of banking, big pharma, the media, and even the education system. Controlling and manipulating the population as "they" see fit to serve them. This ultimate power goes all the way back to the British royal family and includes almost every U.S. president, who have been related or tied to the royal family from the very beginning—all but one, of course. But even that whole trump card could also just be another great show of divide and conquer.

These royal elites learned early that whoever controls the money controls the world. They even make up all the rules, conveniently loaning out money that is not real. Then "they" turn around and loan out more money based on "your debt," which is now an "asset" for the bank—basically doubling the debt yet making profit while doing it. Ah yes, the world of money and central banking—and it all leads back to oil.

Snake oil to be exact.

One of the stories behind John D. Rockefeller is that his father was a traveling snake oil salesman. He was a peddler who sold his miracle herbal potions. I can only guess this had something to do with why herbal remedies became obsolete. He was a con artist who lied and stole from his customers, as well as lying to his own children—to teach them his way. John Rockefeller learned quickly and went on to own and operate Standard Oil Corporation. He also learned early to buy his way out of his poor reputation by purchasing the newspaper, controlling the media. He then went on to control the banking and almost every aspect of our lives, often in the name of charity, when actually the intentions behind the giving were to gain power, money, and control. These "charitable contributions," and those running them, have been decimating small countries for decades.

This is the root of the darkness that currently plagues the earth, but nobody really wants to turn over the big BLACK ROCK to see who is hiding there.

37

A WELL SOUL

Although things were going well with my youngest, my oldest daughter and I were still fairly estranged. It had been over ten years since we had connected much. I had seen her three or four times in the last six years. I missed out on her high school graduation, and college too. Dave had said he just could not condone my coming. He'd strongly suggested I not show up. He didn't want me to ruin her day, he said. He urged me to respect her wishes. She still had me blocked on every possible communication avenue. In December, I sent her an email wishing her Merry Christmas and telling her I had gifts for her.

Her response was not much of a surprise. I should have been used it by now, but it still hurt.

"Take your pills and admit you're bipolar—you know the ultimatum I gave you. The ball has been in your court this entire time. If anyone can understand that it's you, with your mom. You should see that pretty clearly and realize it's a similar situation. Really unfortunate you couldn't break that chain, but I don't fault you for it. I just need to not have you in my life, in order to protect myself—children need stability and support; you gave me neither. And don't bother sending me gifts, I just throw them in the trash."

I guess at least she was communicating. I had taken the prescribed lithium years ago when Sam had first delivered her ultimatum, but even after I did, she still didn't want to see me. So after a few months I stopped. It didn't do much for me—besides, I was already numb. I'd never felt I'd had a bipolar episode. I knew I'd had a spiritual awakening, and yes, I had been very depressed. Who wouldn't be without their children?

"Remember, Sam, forgiveness is a gift you give to yourself," I replied.

After I got Sam's message, I called the doctor who had done a psychiatric evaluation on me years before. I asked for a full evaluation, a new one.

"Give me the meds," I said, "whatever I need."

I was done with the labeling; I didn't care what people would call me. I'd rather have a relationship with my first-born daughter.

I picked up her presents from her dad's. Both she and the trash were undeserving of the contents of the packages. I also took my hairdresser's advice and mentally wrapped up my pain like a present. It was smaller now. I visually wrapped it with smooth matte-black wrapping paper and a bright gold bow. I would keep the small, imaginary box of pain with her Christmas presents in the top of the closet, where I hid some of my gems. My sweet daughter—she was in my heart. I would wait, I would be patient. Maybe she, unlike me, would be the stronger one. Maybe she would break this painful mother-daughter chain. Maybe I reminded her of her own pain, her cancer, because I carried around so much worry and concern. Maybe not seeing me also helped her avoid her own pain.

The doctor's evaluation came back. It was not what I had expected.

The evaluation read:

Client is a 55-year-old divorced white female with a past history of treatment for depression and anxiety. She had 2 very brief hospital stays in 2008 and 2010, initiated or provoked by her ex-spouse while they were going through a divorce. She did not receive any medications at those hospital stays. She spent the next few years trying to gain at least partial custody of her daughters, but was unsuccessful. She feels this contributed to her becoming depressed, and she was eventually treated for depression and anxiety. She reports taking Zoloft for about 3 years, found it helpful. Eventually came off meds 3 years ago, and has been doing well ever since. She was not on a mood stabilizer while on antidepressants, which implies the treating MD did not suspect she had a Bipolar illness. That she took an antidepressant alone for 3 years, without precipitating a mania, is also further evidence that she does not have a Bipolar illness. She has a normal MSE [I had to google to find out that it meant mental status evaluation] currently, as she did when examined 4 years ago by this MD. There have been no clear episodes of mania, including when she had her 2 brief hospital stays back in 2008/2010. That she was not treated with any medications at the time and released quickly, further mitigates against the possibility of her having a Bipolar Illness.

Client appears stable, in a euthymic state. She does not appear to have a Bipolar Illness based on her past history, 2 brief hospital stays with no evidence of mania, 3 years of treatment with an antidepressant alone, with no manias, and her continued euthymic state off meds the past 3 years.

Therefore, suggest client maintain on no medications. She can check in periodically or if any signs of significant mood changes do occur.

Euthymic, which I also looked up, means a neutral mood state. It suggests a person is functional without necessarily being happy or sad. It is defined as a normal or tranquil mental state.

A well soul.

38

HIDDEN IN PLAIN SIGHT

FEBRUARY 2021

Like most things in the world, signs of deep knowledge are hidden in plain sight. Even here in the United States, the mysterious Georgia Guidestones certainly are not hidden. This collection of five enormous granite structures is often referred to as the "American Stonehenge." A post-apocalyptic guide as to how the world should be run is inscribed on these giant slabs, which are perfectly placed to align with the stars and sun. Population control is number one of their ten dictates, which are written in eight languages. Keep the population under five hundred million. That number is quite jolting and a far cry from the 7.8 billion or so that currently reside on the planet. These huge, engraved stones are a perfect astronomical guide of the sun and stars and have many mysteries behind them. Nobody even knows who commissioned the building of the structure. Whoever they were, the anonymous architects certainly knew what they were doing. Not only were these giant monuments built with exact precision to track the sun, serving as a compass, a clock, and a calendar, but they were also meant to be a guide to the New World Order. A one-world government. Could this giant monument be the warning sign to humanity? If "they" warn us ahead of time about what they are doing, does this possibly serve as some sort of consent from society? Is this why everything is in plain sight?

I was contemplating just that as I got up to look for one of my favorite books for inspiration, Nancy Blair's *The Book of Goddesses*. This small book is full of mythical goddesses from around the world and had been my friend and guide for many years. I laughed as I opened to one of my favorite goddesses, never having made all the connections in the past. I then got up and ran to my closet, pulling out one of my favorite sweatshirts, one I hadn't worn in years. On my sweatshirt, just like right then, the captain said, was the Japanese goddess Amaterasu, sitting among the cherry blossoms that were just like the ones tattooed on my arm.

I read again about Goddess Amaterasu. How many times had I read it? The story of Amaterasu, the sun goddess of the Shinto pantheon who hid in a rock cave of Heaven, leaving a darkness on the land. Once she realized she held the light as well as the darkness, she came out from the dark to celebrate her solar self. The light was restored, and there was no need for dualistic ideology. She was the sun and the moon, the dark and the light. I sat back in meditation, in gratitude, looking out through the brand-new windows in my Encinitas apartment.

It was January, and my windows had just been installed on 1/11. I laughed. It may not have been the 1111 window, but it was close enough for me. I smiled as I put the goddess book neatly back on my altar. I hadn't even noticed my name hidden in plain sight within hers. Her last name was also similar to mine, as her name ended in kami.

Amaterasu Omikami.

The circle, the reflection, the connection, the universe—it just never ends.

I reread the affirmation from Nancy Blair's book:

"I am the Sun, and I am the Moon. I release dualistic thinking that confines my potential.

I can be anything I want to be."

"i am kami."

I recited this affirmation again, this time with much more meaning, as I lit the candles on my altar and sat in silent prayer, thanking the universe for my determination to persevere. The goal of the Shinto religion—the "Kami"—is to obtain a pure heart. To embrace the darkness as well as the light.

I was ready to step out of the darkness like that of the cave that had become my life. I picked up my gold rock, the one that was sitting on the little gold book *The Hidden Words*, which also held more than its share of coincidences, also hidden in plain sight.

Years ago, I was chatting on the phone with the shaman friend who I had been working with. He wanted to know if I had ever studied the Baha'i faith. I hadn't really studied it, but I had read through the many Baha'i books that I'd received when I visited the island of Molokai with Dave.

"Hmm," he said, "Well, you are supposed to read a small book called *The Hidden Words*." Looking over at the table next to me, I saw the exact same small book. He had never been to my house, so there was no way he could have known. We had never had a conversation about the Baha'i faith. How would he know *The Hidden Words* sat right next to me, and what did this book mean? It was tiny, less than fifty pages, with a gold cover with a black-and-white bird on it. As asked, I read it again, still not finding the meaning within it. I then picked up my favorite gold rock, a large piece of pyrite that I had gotten the day I went to the loon years ago. I looked at the book again, then at the rock. The rock was exactly the same color as the little golden book. I put the rock on top of the words, and they perfectly covered the title, "The Hidden Words." The bird now appeared to sit on the jagged gold rock. Wasn't that also what my name meant? Kami, the Shinto—the hidden energy of nature in everything? I looked at the book and the bird sitting amongst the cherry blossoms on the cover, and then I saw it.

Oh my GOD. How did I have this little book all these years and never see it? I hurriedly put the book and the rock next to my left arm, next to the tattoo that I'd gotten the first year I opened my store—my bluebird of happiness, I called it. It sat in a tree of cherry blossoms next to a jagged rock. The jagged rock perfectly matched the pyrite rock, which also totally hid "The Hidden Words." The two birds reflected one another, mine blue-and-white, the one on the book black-and-white. Both sat amongst the cherry blossoms. Everywhere I moved the book, the branches of the tree matched those of my tattoo, connecting perfectly as if planned. I looked down in disbelief at the connection of this little book, my rock, and my tattoo. Under the tree on my arm, I had tattooed the word *breathe*. Even the scrolls of the cursive writing perfectly matched up with the scrolls of the design on the little book.

On my other wrist was the word *Grace*, reminding me when I sat in my meditation to breathe Grace, Breathe with God.

"Breathe Grace, Kami—Breathe Grace," they all said, reminding me to breathe and trust in God—in my God-self.

I looked at the birds, reflecting one another, one from heaven and one here on earth, there on my arm. They were just like the heart I wore on my sleeve, my willingness to bare my soul to find the inner answer. But we already knew the answer—it had been told to us over and over again in many spiritual texts.

As above so below.

Every spiritual text says about the same thing if you look very closely. With love and an attitude of oneness, we really can create a positive environment for ourselves and others. This "New Earth" that Eckhart Tolle talks about really is possible—one of freedom, love, healing, and Higher Consciousness. I feel like we are on the verge. We are creating our reality all the time, and we don't even realize it.

This beauty and possibility of oneness is right here, available to us yet hidden right in plain sight because we are not awakened to our own power.

Unity and love are the answers, and division and fear are the weapons in this current spiritual war.

One of my favorite quantum physicists, Michio Kaku, also says, "We don't really want to know the real true story of who we are. It's really quite complicated, and yet simple, we are all aspects of one another. I am you and you are me, we're multidimensional."

Everything is connected. We are all connected and all reflections of one another, whether we believe it or not. Everything we believe, we do indeed receive.

39

TRUST IN THE STARS

I t had been six months since my astrology reading. The astrologer had been right, both about the inheritance and that we would have to work for it. The other people who were splitting the inheritance with my siblings and me were contesting our shares. They argued that my mother had never been adopted by my grandma Barb. So she wasn't, and now we weren't, entitled to the money. The paperwork was inches thick, and I really tried to read between the lines—to understand what it all meant. Lucky for me, I had a good friend, Jan, who was an attorney. I asked her to look at the hefty stack. Had the information about an inheritance and the need to work for it not been in my astrology reading, I probably wouldn't have paid such close attention, and we would have missed the upcoming court date.

Jan hooked me up with a young trust attorney in her office; his family was also from Utah. He offered to take us on without a retainer.

"On your good name, because of Jan, and your Utah ties," he said. "Just don't tell anyone."

A few weeks later he showed up on the Zoom court, all dapper with his perfectly combed blonde hair and bright blue eyes—such a clean-cut Utah boy. He swiftly won the case for us. We had needed a California attorney as the trust was in Napa, where my aunt had lived. He was so good that he even got the initial trust to pay for his fees. Then, we had to hire a Utah attorney to do all the paperwork from our mom's trust, to write up agreements and so on. This time my siblings split the bill for the retainer. Finally, six months later, my siblings and I were about to receive a check each for $40,000. The universe really did show up in crazy, unseen ways.

Once again, I smiled in gratitude as I shook my head. It wasn't enough to live on, my astrologer was right. But it was enough for a little reprieve from my financial burden and to work on my manuscript.

I booked a one-way ticket to Mexico. I wanted to go to see the shadow of the snake during the equinox at Chichen Itza and come to terms with my own shadow-self and the one trying to shadow the world.

40

THE EQUINOX IN MAYA LAND

MARCH 21, 2021

The "Maya" means the illusion of what we fondly call life. I figured it was a great place to go. I wanted to get to the bottom of this illusion of mine, work on my shadow self, and finish this book while also seeing the shadow of the snake at the revered temple.

Ever since that time on the plane flying over Chichen Itza on the equinox, I had wanted to go back. My inheritance had shown up on March 11, my friend Stacey's birthday. I had told myself that if it came before the equinox I would go. Elizabeth, the astrologer, said I should quit my job running my business. I hadn't really needed to do that, as there wasn't a whole lot to quit since I was barely working during the pandemic. Over the past year, I had bought a bigger van, a big Ford Transit that you could stand up in, hoping this would revive my once-again struggling business. Roberto, of course, helped me pimp it out to perfection. We hung little crystal sconces on the walls; clothing bars and an antique table I had brought from Seattle were now bolted to the wall, which was covered in mod, black-and-white floral wallpaper. The pandemic had taken its toll on all small businesses across the country. For once I was grateful to be a "tiny business" without the overhead of a brick-and-mortar store.

I was finally able to pop up again weekly at the local farmers' market because it was outdoors. But gone were the home parties and pop-ups at spas, hair salons, and gyms where I had done most of my business.

God forbid a girl wanted to get her hair or nails done—not here in California—that was taboo during the pandemic. You might infect a person in a small salon, but you could shop at Walmart, Target, and other big-box stores all you wanted. Nothing made much sense to me. Life was changing for many quite rapidly. I had reinvested almost every penny I had for the last three years since my $800 initial investment—I was proud of the progress I had made. When the pandemic hit, I bought the bigger van so I could still try to work by accommodating one-on-one shopping. I had been super frugal over the years, barely buying food and essentials for myself—except for marijuana and hard kombucha. A margarita once in a while and a little champagne were about all the alcohol I could tolerate. Even though my body didn't love alcohol, I still loved the social aspect of ordering a cocktail while out with friends. I would look forward to a good margarita and some deep contemplation.

Even though I'd been excited to go to Mexico, I boarded the plane to Cancun almost reluctantly. I was reluctant because my plan was to finish my memoir there. I had been panicking for days about this and spending so much money on the trip. Also, I had hotels booked for only the first two nights. Usually I loved to just be in the flow and see how things would unfold, but this time I was nervous about my sudden plan to take this trip. It felt so carefree and excessive during the pandemic that I almost felt guilty.

I also needed to focus and finish this book. Writing at home in my apartment often seemed impossible. I could always find an excuse to vacuum or clean out a drawer. Now, with a stack of pages of tedious revisions, I boarded the plane eager to focus and write.

I flew to Cancun and rented a car. And no, I do not speak Spanish. I stayed the first night in the smallest of the giant hotels I could find close to the airport. The next morning, I swam in the beautiful turquoise water, laid in the sun for an hour, and headed to Chichen Itza, three hours away. I couldn't find my next hotel, the Hotel Okaan. The GPS kept trying to tell me to turn left on a road that wasn't there.

This is not unlike my life, I thought. "Why do I always choose the hard road?" I said out loud to myself.

I finally found it my third time back and forth on the road. The hotel was not well marked—and it was all the way up a dirt road into the jungle. I kept wondering if I should turn around. Thankfully, I didn't, as I fell in love with the place instantly.

The entire place felt like a sanctuary. It was surrounded by a shallow, sprawling pool with perfectly cut, narrow wood branches forming a path around it, connecting it to the wild jungle where it was nestled. There were meandering paths and bridges, one that led to a hollowed-out pool in the middle with big rocks for chairs that surrounded a large teepee stack of prepped wood for a bonfire. There was a circle for fire ceremonies and a meditation platform that sat on stilts. Hand-carved wooden pillars jutted out from the shallow pool, which held black fringed hammocks that swung slightly in the wind. The entrance to this area also had a row of giant, carved wooden beams that came together as upside down V shapes. Round, hand-woven twig lamps hung from each one. I was in the middle of the jungle with barely any cell phone service and no TVs—just peace, quiet, and tranquility. In the open-air, thatched restaurant hung many crocheted and feathered dream catchers and Mexican stained-glass lamps. A large cluster of metal star lamps and a few heart-shaped ones made from twigs hung in the middle of the restaurant.

Plants were everywhere—large vines with leaves bigger than your head wound their way up the palm trees. I was swooning over the decor and lush beauty of this sanctuary.

I had only been checked in for a few minutes, and already I'd been to the pool for a quick dip and returned to a beautiful, pink hammock hanging from my deck, which overlooked the sanctuary pool. I looked around at all the other hammocks—mine was the only pink one that I could see. Smiling at the hammock in my favorite color, I went back to the office and told them I might want to stay a couple more days. Then I drove to Chichen Itza.

It was late afternoon, the nineteenth of March, The Day. It was the equinox, the day I had been waiting so long for. Only on the equinox could you see the shadow of the snake going to the sides of the temple as the sun hit the revered pyramid at sunset.

I drove the short distance, parked, and walked in. I had heard it might be closed to the public, but it hardly looked closed—it was packed!

As I followed the road that led to the temple, a guy stopped me at the entrance.

"Hey, Lady! We closed."

"Closed? What do you mean closed?" I asked.

"Yes, we close at four. Now we are closed for three days," he said.

I stood there, dumbfounded, I didn't know what to say or do. I walked down the road for a while watching all the people streaming from the place. There were rows and rows of motorcycles with men ready to give people a ride into the temple, I guessed.

I walked up and asked one of them,

"Is it really closed, and for three days?"

"Yes," he said, "but you can come back at seven for the light show!"

Oh right, I had heard about that. I had come all this way to see the shadow of the snake, and instead of a shadow I got a light show. Because of the pandemic and the huge crowds of people who usually frequented the place, they had decided to close. Hadn't I seen enough shadows? How about some light for a change?

To pass the time until the light show, I went into the small town and had an amazing buffet of chilaquiles, chicken, rice, and tortillas. At the restaurant, I happily watched two beautiful women dance with beer bottles on their heads. Next, they danced with whole trays of glasses, and the beer bottles, on their heads.

Wasn't that what Paramahansa had said to me long ago? "Anything is possible with balance."

I smiled at the pretty ladies, who were entertaining everyone. Aside from me, there was only one other large group in the restaurant: thirty or forty people all wearing white with lavender sashes or trim. I wasn't sure if they were celebrating someone or celebrating the equinox. It was a pretty big deal around here.

After dinner, I drove the short distance back to the temple to see the light show. It was incredible seeing the temple and all the smaller buildings surrounding it all lit up at night. Before the show, we got to tour the entire grounds. I couldn't have been more delighted as I walked around the temple and its surrounding buildings, which were all lit up with green, red, and blue lights casting their own colorful shadows onto the giant lawns that surrounded the place. It was a small group, under fifty, and we had the place to ourselves as we settled into the small grouping of folding chairs to watch the show. Getting to see the temple in the day would have been a thrill—but this light show under the stars was more than I could have hoped for. The lights and show were serene and magical as the lights danced upon the giant temple of Chichen Itza.

The next day, I sat by the pool. I alternated writing with reading *Between the World and Me*, by Ta-Nehisi Coates, which was wonderful, raw, and poetic. I was inspired and moved by the eloquent view of the world he shared with his son, and what it feels like being a black man in today's world. I pretty much had the place to myself, except for one couple. I said hello and struck up a conversation. They were staying at the hotel for an equinox ceremony and had twenty or so people in their group. To call it Shangri-la would not have been a mistake.

Even though they lived nearby, the couple had decided to stay to enjoy the property while their group toured a different nearby temple. Their names were Nacho and Stella. She was from Columbia, and he was from Mexico, yet they had traveled and lived in several countries for the past thirty years. His name was Ignacio, but they called him Nacho for short.

"Oh," I said, "so you are only one chip?"

He chuckled.

Stella didn't think I seemed like I was from California, whatever that meant. She wanted to know if I was vaccinated and if I liked Biden—politics and religion, and we were already talking about the vaccination. These topics caused fear, control, and division in my mind. I already knew to tread lightly on these particular subjects, so I hesitated, not wanting to answer. I had leaned towards Western medicine my whole life. I had just had surgery. Some members of my spiritual community had shamed me for choosing Western medicine for the healing of my child. But it had saved her. I had always followed Western medicine, but something about the vaccine did not sit well with me, and I wasn't sure why.

I just laughed and changed the subject, telling the couple how much I loved, loved, loved this place.

"I couldn't believe they knew my favorite color was pink, giving me a pink hammock." Stella, the beautiful, vibrant woman, replied, "Oh, it is not accidental, these people are very aware—not one thing around here is accidental. It is all in perfect flow."

I felt this statement was profound. I mean, isn't everything in the universe actually in perfect flow? I liked her already and asked her if she had ever read *How Stella Got Her Groove Back*. She hadn't.

She then answered for me.

"Well, we are not vaccinated. We do not believe in the vaccination—and we think Biden is a reptilian!" I burst out laughing, not because I agreed with her but because it was funny. Funny because how long had it been since I had even heard the term reptilian? I wasn't interested in going down the rabbit hole with them over this topic, which contrary to what people thought, actually had nothing to do with politics. However, I loved how open they were and that they believed in living in unison with Mother Earth. I asked Nacho if he was Mayan.

He said, "Maybe, but maybe the Mayans are not from here. Maybe they are extraterrestrial and went back home."

I loved contemplating such things and looked forward to cracking open some of these topics a bit more when I returned home, but for now I was grateful for the peace, the solace, and laughter and connection with new friends.

We met up later on the sungazing deck. It was open to everyone, but we were the only ones there. I was dressed all in white for my own personal ceremony, paying tribute to the sun. It was absolutely beautiful out as the big, bright orange sun began to set in the trees just next to the top of the revered temple that you could see from the hotel. They said I should stay a few more days, and I agreed. This really was heaven, and why would I want to leave anyway? I mean, I did love the white sandy beaches and turquoise water of Tulum, but there was just something magical about the jungle. After they left, I meditated, then looked down next to the concrete jaguar bench. I mean, how did they get that up here? Or was it made up here? This place was so mysterious; the only other thing on the deck was a half-carved wood stick. It was three-feet-long, carved on one end, and cut raw-edged on the other. A dancing stick, I thought. It fit between my hands and was perfectly shoulder width. I felt compelled to dance under the amazing stars with the heavy stick. I imagined it to be a magic shaman stick as I danced and blessed the earth. It was gorgeous out, and so dark that you could see every last star. I went back to my room to swing on my pink hammock on the patio. I looked up and saw an odd, cutout, arch-shaped overhang. It was made up of half of an arch over part of my room and another half arch over the room next door.

Curious, I looked up. The big dipper was *right there*, visible between the two arched cutouts like a spoon laying on the wall between the arches. Was this, too, planned out? That's how the Mayan people were. Everything fit perfectly. The raw rock walls were perfectly stacked together, big rocks with small ones interlocking to make the walls that formed the path all along the dirt roads of the place. They had no concrete holding them together. Everything amazed me. I went downstairs, splurged, and had another margarita. Life was pretty magical.

Later that night, I watched as Stella and Nacho's group came back from the *cenote*, an underground pool of water where they had been all day, holding their ceremony. I got to watch as one by one they walked around the sanctuary pool, all dressed in white, of course, carrying candles over the bridge and into the empty middle pool for the fire ceremony. It was beautiful and in Spanish, so I didn't understand the chants, but it didn't matter; I was so happy to be part of this beautiful energy. When I went to bed, they were still praying and chanting below. I fell asleep and swore I was waking up to the ancient drum of the Mayan people. I even got up and looked out from the balcony, and the group was still there. It was almost eleven p.m., and their ceremony was obviously winding down, but I could still hear drums—but they were not coming from this group. I even went upstairs to the sundeck, but it was quiet. Yet, I could still hear drums. We were in the middle of nowhere. It was probably someone in one of the darling bungalows below.

The next morning, I woke up early as I had been doing. It was barely light as I went upstairs to the sundeck to watch the sunrise. I was soon followed by my new friends' entire group for a sunrise ceremony. I hadn't known they were planning this, and I couldn't really leave as the narrow, winding staircase was full of them all coming up. I had met a couple of the women just moments before who told me their group had been "charging" crystals in sacred sites and then burying them. Apparently, I wasn't the only one burying crystals around the world with the intention of activating the sacred ley lines—to raise the vibration of the planet. They were somewhat disappointed that they didn't get to bury them close to the temple, but they planned to charge them on the jaguar altar bench with the sunrise and salutation. They invited me to stay. They had "checked in with the priestess" who was leading their group, they said. They saw me panic and try to leave. She had said it was okay, I could stay. So, I did. Soon my new friends Stella and Nacho came up the stairs.

"Hi, Stella, Hi, One Chip," I said.

They chuckled and hugged me. It was absolutely beautiful, and after forty-five minutes of prayer, meditation, and sungazing, I snuck down the winding stairs quietly in my pink cherry-blossom slippers, still in my pajamas.

I worked on my memoir for a few hours, then did my daily walk to the office to ask for *una noche más*, one more night. This had been my morning ritual every day for the past few days. I just couldn't leave.

Stella and Nacho were in the office checking out. We talked for a bit, then they left and came back to ask if I wanted to have a drink with them.

"Ah sure, but it's a little early for drinks for me."

I was still kind of recovering from my drinks the day before, from splurging on three margaritas.

"No alcohol," they laughed.

"Just a *Jimica*," Nacho said.

"Okay. That I can do." I said.

We went back to the restaurant, which had been packed earlier when I'd been writing in a quiet corner. They hadn't even seen me earlier—my head lost in my computer. They wanted to let me know that I was on a good journey. They could see me.

"Trust and listen," Stella said.

They also reminded me to go to the cenote close by and walk the path behind my room. "There is a temple there, on the grounds. You will love it," Nacho said.

I hugged Nacho, the quiet Mayan, and then Stella, who I thanked for "helping me get my groove back," helping me to step into my knowing and trust in myself. It was nice to be "seen." My heart really was full of good intentions.

I got ready and went to the cenote, which was close by. This was my fourth time to the Yucatan, and I had never been to a cenote. These underground bodies of water made from collapsing limestone are in hollowed-out circles, oftentimes hundreds of feet below the surface. This cenote had vines hanging from nearby trees, deep into the water. There were natural springs and waterfalls that constantly replenished the hole with water.

In the past, cenotes were often sites of sacrificial offerings. They are sacred to the people of the Yucatan. You have to wash your feet and even the bottoms of your shoes as you walk into the area, then you walk through some kind of decontaminating spray. If you want to swim, you have to shower first and wear a life jacket. Then you walk down the long, steep rock stairs to the cave. Halfway down, my right kneecap began to buckle. It hurt so badly I could hardly get down the stairs.

My hotel room was on the third floor, and I had been going up and down the stairs for days and nothing. Now it hurt, like crazy, but I really wanted to go swim—so I persisted. I am a good swimmer, and I had a life jacket, but the dark, cold water scared me. It was 150 feet deep or more. I pushed myself and boldly kicked out to the middle of the circle, where the vines came down to the water. The trees went up from the water, growing next to the immense, rock cave walls, reaching hundreds of feet up. It was stunning, like what I had always imagined inner earth might look like. This feeling is almost as powerful as meeting Ayahuasca herself, I thought. The vines wrapped around the trees that sank into the brisk water. I was amazed at the sun glistening on the cold, dark water as trickles came down from the vines, forming endless ripples. I lay back and floated in the middle of the circle and wept. The tears would not stop. I was so overcome by the tranquil beauty of this magical place. How had I never been to a cenote? I stayed until I was shivering. The water was quite cold in the deep cavernous pit. I walked back up, and my knee was fine.

I vowed to go back down. So I got a snack at the restaurant up top, then went back. At the same spot, my knee gave out again, but I stumbled down, determined to get back in the sacred water. Four women were in the middle of the circle of water holding hands in prayer. It seemed that everywhere I went, people were in celebration and prayer here—I was grateful. I went to the middle, laid back, and silently chanted my favorite prayer, the Gayatri Mantra. Here I was, deep within the earth in a sacred pool. Again, I wept. I felt the presence of Aya, the root of Mother Earth, more than ever. I felt enveloped by the rich darkness, as if this were the place that the dark queen herself held court. I later learned that cenotes are known to be pools to the underworld.

I left the cenote wet and a bit dazed. The water made my hair so curly that I was surprised at how good it looked without a brush to comb out its craziness. I got dressed and went looking for the temple on the property and soon found it. It was an outdoor structure with wooden floors and curtains on the sides and some shades. A big Buddha stood on the altar along with a statue of Mother Mary. There was a big, open cross cut into the wall to see outside into the jungle. I could only imagine what it might look like with the light shining through. Everything here was in perfect, planned precision. The place was simple, serene, and beautiful. Because Mother Mary was there, I felt Jesus was somehow missing. This was a Mayan temple, after all. I walked all over the place singing the Gayatri Mantra once again, wondering what it would be like to hold ceremony there. I sat down in meditation, then lay back on the rug overwhelmed with bliss. I looked up and saw him. Jesus was there on a cross nestled above the rafters. Under his feet hung a blue evil eye symbol, meaning protection. I laughed again, as Jesus always seemed to show up. Jesus, for me, was an unconditional reflection of love. Nothing was missing.

At dinner, as usual behind my computer, I wrote as I ate a plate of rich seafood crepes. The big group had left, but another smaller group was having dinner. The young, cute girl who I had said hello to briefly the night before with her boyfriend on the sundeck stopped at my table to say hi.

"Are you having fun?" I asked.

The look on her face said it all, even before she answered.

"Well, we are here for an Ayahuasca ceremony."

Fun was hardly a term for an Ayahuasca experience, as I well knew.

"You have a trusted shaman, yes?" I asked.

"Oh yes, he has been practicing for thirty years," the young girl replied.

"Okay, good," I breathed, relieved.

I had worried about how trendy the sacred ritual had become. This kind of ceremony was not something one should do without a seriously trained shaman. No wonder I had not seen this crew. Maybe these were the drums I had heard?

I had been feeling and thinking of Aya all day, something I hadn't done in years. I felt honored to hear her, feel her, and swim in her dark waters. All without having to drink of her vile truth serum, which could be like years of therapy but felt awful while in the process and preparation. She was here—I was not alone; I had the biggest mama ever looking over me. Stella was right, I was on a good journey. My journey was not for everyone, but I knew I was where I was supposed to be.

I would not give up waiting for my own little chicken to find her way back.

I release my pain and share this story. I am hardly a chicken shit.

I am hard, like my stone egg—nothing will crack me.

41

THE OUROBOROS

My lips had been peeling for over a month. I had used oral meds, and topicals of every kind. My lips throbbed and would not stop. It hurt to eat, talk, or laugh. I attributed it to the fact that this storytelling was coming to life. Soon my truth would be told. My skin would be pulled back, my underbelly of wounds and theories would be open for judgment. Maybe just like the snake, I literally needed to shed my skin, shed my old story.

I still lacked that spark that had captivated me the day I left for the loon. That day seemed so long ago, yet still felt so surreal. Life in that incident was unlike any drug or high I had ever been on in my life.

It was so real; I knew it existed. Yet that energy was still not part of my current reality. I just needed to look a little further. The thin veil was right in front of me, clouding my vision and dampening my vibe. The grey, dark clouds that constantly hung over my tiny apartment by the beach certainly were not helping. May Grey, June Gloom, then it was July and now August, now what? August Smogest? I felt I shouldn't complain about the grey as fires raged across the land, making most places grey with unhealthy air. The fire and poor air quality helped to further the fear that raged across nation.

It felt as though the *Hunger Games* movies really and truly were being played out. "We"—being most of society, were the current players as the elites of the world sat back and watched—knowing they had been playing us for over a century now. It was time for society to wake up.

This grey weather and the fear-based consciousness were really starting to get the best of me. It felt like endless months of ugly fearmongering and ugly, grey weather. I longed for that spark of life, the energy that inspires us. The connection.

I am always so grateful for my work and the connections I make there. Maybe that's why I like working so much. Work is where I found connection, found my people.

I recently met a customer who wanted me to order her a kimono. She handed me her card, which said she was an Akashic reader. I had never met an Akashic reader before, well, except for myself, of course. However, I hadn't been able to do much reading as I'd gotten my ass kicked out of that library. Or had I somehow always tiptoed in? I had always known we could tap into higher dimensions of learning, or of ourselves. I hadn't really known why. I just kind of knew. It was through vibration and eye connection that I knew. Those who knew, just knew. I could always sense people like that, and usually they could sense me as well. But I was still lacking that underlying luster, the spark. No amount of alcohol or drugs or ceremonies or prayers had gotten me there.

Only connection could, and I longed for that.

I made an appointment with my customer for an Akashic reading and met her with two kimonos in hand. I realized how funny this was as they are inspired by a Japanese robe. Another recent Luv thing fave, a Kimono literally means "a thing to wear." My customer, Lynn, loved her kimonos, but I could tell she was a bit nervous, and she was holding back things she didn't want to say.

She said she had to be honest with me and say that she had never heard of souls like mine before and that she, herself, had needed to look it up.

I was a parallel soul.

Again, I just shook my head in disbelief as once again I heard my own story. This time of my soul's existence.

Parallel souls could see the other side; they were empathetic and sensitive, often feeling the collective pain.

Wow, wasn't that more than true.

Apparently, there were not many parallel souls here on the planet, as the energy was too dense here and most died before the age of two. Very few lived long lives.

Ah, a lightbulb moment—that was probably why I had the big scar at my groin. It was why I had spent so much time in the hospital as a baby and nobody had known what was wrong with me. I knew it was my determination that had saved me. Again, I quietly shook my head as Lynn paused once again, not wanting to tell me of the discomfort most souls like myself often feel.

So, I blurted it out. "So, they kill themselves?"

"Yes," she said, looking down at her hands.

The pain and suffering on the planet were just too much for most; however, it felt it was my job to help shed some light.

Thanks, I said, no pressure. Try not to kill yourself, and also help wake up the planet from the people who have been monopolizing every single aspect of the world for close to a century.

This was my 1111, and I could see through the window.

It was as if I could see this land beyond the illusion of this current state—a land where we really and truly let down the walls of division and fear and let our minds and hearts fall into oneness.

I knew it to be true—this beauty, this "other life," this other dimension. I just knew of its possibility. This knowing was not of this land, yet it was. It was just beyond this dimension, or possibly beyond our—this—ILLUSION! Or possibly the parallel one.

OUR COLLECTIVE MOVIE.

And then I fucking got it. The Snake ate its own tail! The great universal oneness.

I looked it up.

Humanity itself is its worst enemy, even if we did not intentionally know it, for this is the great cycle of life.

The good and the bad—both in perfect perfection—Duality.

The Ouroboros is an ancient symbol depicting a snake eating its own tail. The circle, or eternal cycle of life, signifies life and death—Duality.

The final copy of this book came back from my editor with the date boldly written at the top of the page. It was my mother's birthday—November 19.

119—I may not be enlightened, but I am unburdened.

And so it is.

EPILOGUE

In a recent discussion regarding this book and my story, I was asked what makes me and this book different.

My response surprised even me. I am not a lightworker, there are plenty of people spreading love and goodness to the world—all of which are needed. However, I am really a *dark* worker. I admitted that I didn't know what a dark worker was and had never even heard the term. It was a customer who sent me to this definition:

In contrast to light workers, there are those who work with the energies of a darker nature. For all that light, there must always be dark in some form, where the light cannot reach. The people who work with this darkness are referred to as dark workers.

Dark workers work with elements deemed dark, such as the dead, crystals (which grow, form, and evolve in darkness—despite having such a light appearance), and varying planes and guides.

To a dark worker, darkness simply means "not light." Dark workers are accustomed to energies of a more shadowy nature, bending them to our wills and caring for those they affect.

Darkness is required to balance light, as everything in life is balanced.

A dark worker is not the opposite of a light worker; rather we are complimentary. While a light worker, such as a Reiki healer, will infuse a person with universal light and energy to flush out darkness, a dark worker draws away the darkness already present, or manipulates it to become more manageable. Dark workers draw the universal light energy up from the earth below through the root chakra.

As energy workers we may perform our functions either consciously, directly drawing darkness, or unconsciously, by counseling those in need. Before "awakening" as a dark worker, we often take on many roles as counselors or protectors, quite subconsciously. As a result, we can take on that darkness and often overwhelm ourselves with it. If not well managed, a dark worker can easily fall into depression and self-harming, either psychic, emotional, or physical.

AUTHOR BIO

Kamie Kay grew up in a small town in Utah. Her early curiosity and trauma seeded her determination to win in the so-called "game of life." Her journey led her to the coast of California, where she believed she was living "the dream," only to find herself waking up in one nightmare after another.

Growing up, people could never pronounce her name—spelled Kamie. As her search for the "I am" continued, she realized that dropping the "E" could symbolize dropping the E-go.

"i am kami" is not just her own story of growth through trauma and awakening, but everyone's story.

Thank you, Mom, and thank you, Mother Gaia

Gayatri Mantra

ॐ भूर्भुवः स्वः
तत्सवितुर्वरेण्यम
भर्गो देवस्य धीमहि।
धियो यो नः प्रचोदयात ॥

Aum
Bhur Bhuvah Svah
Tat Savitur Varenyam
Bhargo Devasya Dheemahi
Dhiyo Yo nah Prachodayat

The Goddess Gayatri represents infinite knowledge.
It is she who eliminates the darkness or ignorance from
our life, helping us to attain enlightenment by
showering us with her wisdom.

*"Gayatri is the Mother of all scriptures (Vedas). She is present,
wherever Her name is chanted. She is very powerful. The One
who nourishes the individual being is Gayatri. She bestows pure
thoughts on anyone who worships Her. She is the embodiment of
all Goddesses. Our very breath is Gayatri, our faith in existence
is Gayatri. Gayatri has five faces, they are the five life principles.
She has nine descriptions, they are 'Om, Bhur, Bhuvah, Swah, Tat,
Savitur, Vareñyam, Bhargo, Devasya.' Mother Gayatri nourishes
and protects every being and she channelizes our senses in the
proper direction. 'Dhīmahi' means meditation. We pray to her to
inspire us with good intelligence. 'Dhīyo Yonah Prachodayāt'—We
beseech her to bestow on us everything we need. Thus Gayatri is a
complete prayer for protection, nourishment and finally, liberation."*
—Sri Sathya Sai Baba,
My Dear Students, Vol 3, Ch 2, Mar 19, 1998,

Made in the USA
Monee, IL
06 August 2022

16b35697-2a47-4b91-a02d-ce30ac6b09b7R01